PONCHO SANCHEZ'
CONGA COOKBOOK

by Poncho Sanchez with Chuck Silverman

To access audio visit:
www.halleonard.com/mylibrary

2165-6467-6540-6873

Poncho Sanchez records exclusively for Concord Picante Records.

Special thanks to Chuck Silverman (for all his knowledge in helping to put this book together), Jim Cassell, David Torres, and Remo Belli. Thanks also to the fine musicians George Lopez (bongos, bell) and René Camacho (bass).

Poncho Sanchez plays Remo El Conguero Series and Poncho Sanchez Signature Series conga drums and uses Remo drum heads.

Website: **www.ponchosanchez.com**

Poncho Sanchez is exclusively represented by
Jim Cassell
The Berkeley Agency
2608 9th St., #301
Berkeley, CA 94710
Phone: 510-843-4902
Fax: 510-843-7271
www.berkeleyagency.com
mail@berkeleyagency.com

Cover and "Conga Basics" photos by Neil Zlozower

ISBN 978-1-57560-363-2

Visit Hal Leonard Online at
www.halleonard.com

Table of Contents

Introduction

Dear Friends and Musicians,

Thanks for taking the time to check out the *Conga Cookbook*. I've been playing music for a long time and many friends have asked me about my style of playing: where it comes from, how I developed it, and my inspirations for playing music. I've never had formal training or lessons—I've just been given a gift and, thankfully, I can share that gift with you!

When I was approached to write a book I had to sit down and think about what I could offer. Really, what I have to give comes from my soul. It comes from the many evenings and mornings that, as a young kid, I would lie in bed and listen to the mambo and *chachachá* records that my sisters were listening to. It comes from playing a lot when I was young, soaking up the sounds from all around me and expressing myself on drums. Most of all, it comes from performing with some really soulful musicians.

I was born in Laredo, Texas, and my whole family—I'm the youngest of 11—moved to Norwalk, California, when I was four. My family listened to great Latin music from Tito Puente to Tito Rodriguez, Celia Cruz to Orquesta Aragón, plus we listened to all of the Eastside sounds like boogaloo and soul and doo-wop. In my house, you could hear it all, including Charlie Parker and Dizzy, and Clifford Brown. We listened to so much Latin music that I thought it was music from Texas!

At first, I played guitar in some bands around my neighborhood. I was in the sixth grade. The guy across the street had a rhythm and blues band and I started to play with them. One band that I joined had four guitarists and they needed a singer—the next thing I knew, I was the lead vocalist. It was "here are the songs, here's a stack of 45s, we've got a gig Saturday, learn them all." That's how I got my vocal training! Since that day I've been the lead vocalist of all the bands I've been in.

Poncho and Ramon Banda

I played a lot, jamming at Griffith Park here in L.A.—we played rumba, conga, *son*, everything, for hours. What an experience! Soon I was working around town, playing with some great musicians. Thanks to them, I really started to develop my sound, as well as a respect for the music.

A great thing happened to me in 1974 when Cal Tjader called me and I joined his band. Our first gig together was New Year's Eve at the Coconut Grove at the Ambassador

In ninth or tenth grade, I got a drum set. I played a little Latin jazz and some straight-ahead jazz as well with a band called the Midnight Set. In the 11th grade, I got my first set of congas—my dad bought one and I bought the other one. All I did was put on my Cal Tjader, Mongo, and Tito Puente records and play along. Soon after this, I saw Mongo Santamaria, Willie Bobo, and Cal Tjader play at the Lighthouse in Hermosa Beach. Mongo really whacked the drums and I knew I wanted to sound like him.

Poncho and Francisco Aguabella

Hotel. Wow! I was with Cal for seven and a half years and I still think of him a lot; it was a great friendship and a wonderful musical time. I learned so much with Cal. I was as green as they come, from the Norwalk barrio. He was my musical father—I idolized and respected him. Most of all, I learned how Cal conducted himself in front of the people, how he'd speak in public. He was very polite and well mannered, with a lot of class. Musically, he would pick certain jazz standards for his tunes. He really could pick 'em—Cal had great taste.

Clare Fischer joined the Tjader group a couple of years later. He's a harmonic genius—very musically complex. I'd hear all of the beautiful voicings and harmonies that Clare would use; I soaked up what I could and I still use what I learned from him to this day. We co-founded the band Salsa Picante. He wanted Salsa Picante to sound *típico* with the sophisticated harmonic jazz influence. It was a really great band and a wonderful experience.

With Cal Tjader

I've had my own band for 20 years now. We've recorded 19 albums, four of which have been nominated for Grammy awards. Wow! All of this from a guy from Laredo, Texas! I see my band growing and playing all different kinds of music, not only Latin jazz and salsa. I'd like to do a tribute to James Brown, the Godfather of Soul, and maybe another tribute to Tito Rodriguez, the great singer from Puerto Rico. We have fun in the band. I think that's what I can bring to this book: How to play congas and have fun doing it. Sure, you have to have some technique and then practice a lot, but having fun and letting your soul free is what I want to bring to you. Thanks for letting me share my soul and my music with you.

Poncho Sanchez
poncho@ponchosanchez.com
http://www.ponchosanchez.com

The Purpose of the Conga Cookbook

This conga drum method has been developed to give you an approachable and easy-to-understand tool to help you to play. The different rhythms examined here all have their own distinctive patterns, feels, and technical challenges. By developing these rhythms, you will enhance your vocabulary and groove and develop the techniques necessary to play all of the styles presented here plus many more. The section on soloing also explores different sounds and techniques. For those of you who enjoy the drumming style of Poncho Sanchez, you'll get even closer to that style now!

No matter what, you'll definitely find your playing improving as you pick up on the nuances that make for a great *conguero*.

The *Conga Cookbook* features play-alongs for each of the styles under study. By listening to each tune with congas, you can get a great idea of the proper feel—then it's your turn! By using the proper sounds and techniques found within this book, you'll be able to fit right into the groove. Just adjust the channels of your sound system so you can play along with the track, either by being the only drummer with the band or with Poncho playing along.

Here is a word about the charts for the play-alongs. The notation provided is very close to what Poncho plays for most of each play-along, but there are variations to these basic grooves. It is most important for you to achieve the proper sound and groove for each basic pattern and then use what you have learned in the preceding chapter to fill out the grooves, adding spice and flavor where and when you want.

Of course, there are the great recipes found throughout the book—use them as rewards! After you've gotten your groove really happening and you've been cookin' with the play-alongs, then you can start *really* cookin' with Poncho's recipes!

Each chapter has many grooves for you to practice. They've been purposefully played at very slow tempos so you can hear each stroke and nuance. After you've spent time practicing, the play-alongs are there for you to try the grooves at performance tempos. Some of the patterns may sound similar to you, but examine them more closely and you'll find that the ways in which they are played are different.

Lastly, Poncho and I both decided that, in order to demonstrate how you can grow from using the *Conga Cookbook*, I would record the exercises for the book. I learned so much myself from transcribing and practicing these grooves!

We hope you enjoy the *Conga Cookbook*.

Chuck Silverman
chuck@chucksilverman.com
http://www.chucksilverman.com

Neil Zlowzower

A History of the Congas

By Dr. Olavo Alén Rodriguez
Center for the Study and Development of Cuban Music, Havana, Cuba
Translated by William H. Phillips
Photos: Center for the Development of Cuban Music, Havana, Cuba

Yuka Drums, Matanzas Province

The conga or *tumbadora* originated as a musical instrument in Cuba as part and parcel of the rumba, yet the instrument is nowhere to be found in the early days of this important Cuban musical genre.

The word rumba was used originally in Cuban music as a synonym for *fiesta*. To "make a rumba" was to throw a party; however, this usage was limited solely to certain segments of the 19th century Cuban populace for, in Cuba, many expressions were used as synonyms for *party*. Farmers in the island's eastern region called their parties *changüí*, whereas farmers in the central and eastern areas called them *guateques*. Many ethnic groups of the complex that nurtured Afro-Cuban music called their parties *tumbas*. For this purpose, other expressions were adopted as well, such as: *bembé, macumbas, mambos* and, of course, *rumbas*.

Rumba as a synonym for *party* was an expression used by a segment of the populace concentrated in the inner-city zones of Havana and Matanzas. These were mainly neighborhoods that harbored unskilled laborers and other economically underprivileged groups.

In 1886, Cuba utterly abolished slavery and the slave trade. Thus, about a quarter of a million individuals obtained their freedom. However, this did little for their economic situations. These people couldn't remain in the country because they weren't the owners of the land. But it was also difficult for them, owing to the scarcity of economic resources, to become city dwellers. The frequent outcome was that such people drifted into the outskirts of several western Cuban cities where they built themselves very rudimentary dwellings out of whatever materials they could lay hands on, or else rented rundown houses where a number of families would all live together. This gave rise to a type of housing known in Cuba by the name of *solar* (slum) or *cuartería*. In these surroundings, the Cuban rumba was born.

The musical instruments on which the rumba was first played were the side board of a cabinet and the emptied and overturned drawer from a dressing table. A pair of spoons served as drumsticks and also to beat rhythms on the bottom of a frying pan taken from the kitchen. The aim was to create a complex cross-rhythm to accompany those who sang and, above all, to liven things up for the dancers.

Bembe Drums, Matanzas Province

From the outset, this *rumba* scenario brought together descendants of widely dissimilar African tribes and peoples who had arrived in Cuba as slaves. Other participants were members of a poor white population who had come to Cuba seeking work and who had become laborers or small business people such as dyers, fruit or meat vendors, and the like.

In these slum neighborhoods, some of the rhythms, styles, and ways of singing and making music began to take on unique characteristics, perhaps because those taking part were from such widely varied backgrounds. Although these festivities certainly had their origins in the slave compound, the new environment lent them a totally new kind of expression, so that *rumba* ceased to be simply another word for *party* and took on the meaning both of a defined Cuban musical genre and also of a very specific form of dance, quite distinct from other strata of Cuba's population.

Regularization through repetition of musical elements, rhythmic and melodic phrasing, and stabilization of highly unique performance styles on improvised musical instruments brought about the birth of a highly original way of making music. However, this crystallized into distinct styles, each with determined mannerisms and particular social and musical behaviors. Thus were born the rumba forms: *guaguancó, yambú, columbia,* and such now-extinct variants as *jiribilla* and *resedá*. What differentiated them was the different ethnic mix of each town, city, or rural locality.

Evolution led to necessary changes, and so the sideboard, drawer, and frying pan were superceded by *cajones* or "boxes" of different sizes which were rumba's first true musical instruments. This must have occurred in the last decades of the 19th century in the provinces of Havana and Matanzas.

The *cajón* is played directly with the hands using both fingers and palms. On occasion, spoons are also used as drumsticks. The largest *cajón* is placed on the ground and the musician sits on it to beat with his hands on the back and one of the sides. The second, smaller-sized *cajón* is placed across the legs of a player seated on a chair or bench. Generally it is beaten on its sides, although the front can also be played. The third *cajón* is the smallest of the ensemble. It is played by holding it between the legs and beating on the upper edge. In this case, nearly the entire instrument is beaten, seeking the best possible range of tones and exploiting the different sounds obtained by striking different points between the center and the edge of the lid. Sometimes the player attaches small tin plates or metal maracas to his wrists, considerably enriching the polyrhythms obtained.

The large and medium *cajones* play repetitive rhythm patterns while the smallest, having the brightest sounds, improvises rhythmic fragments and variations of striking virtuosity. A fourth player is frequently found playing with two spoons on one side of the large *cajón* or some other object a repetitive rhythm in the high frequency range which serves occasionally to keep time for the group.

The largest *cajón* is often called the *salidor*, the mid-sized one the *tres-dos*, and the smallest the *quinto*. Evidently, these names allude to the functions each one fulfills in producing the characteristic cross-rhythms of rumba.

The *cajones* are therefore the historical precursors of the *tumbadoras* (congas) in the rumba fiesta. However, the congas' natural forebears are from a very different sort of place.

We have observed a marked morphological similarity between the oldest forms of the conga drum and the *ngoma* drum. Likewise, there are resemblances to various versions of the *makuta* drums. Most important perhaps is the barrel shape of the drum; moreover the fact that both the *ngoma* and *makuta* drums have heads of tacked-on cowhide makes them likely ancestors of the Cuban conga drum. The first *tumbadoras* had their skins or heads tacked directly to the upper opening of the shell in a manner similar to drums brought by people of Congo or Bantu origin to Cuba.

Makuta Drums, Matanzas Province

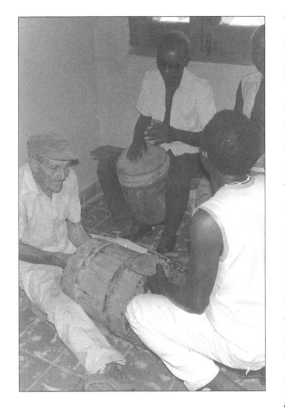

The *ngoma* drums, also known as *palo* ("stick") drums, were the instruments used in ceremonies and celebrations of the Palo Order. This religion was brought to Cuba by various ethnic groups of the Bantu peoples. The *ngoma* ensemble may have two, three, or four drums of different sizes which together produce complicated cross-rhythms. In general, these drums are barrel-shaped, although sometimes they may also be of a tubular, cylindrical shape. They have a single head stretched over the upper opening while the lower end is open. The head is tacked to the wooden body of the instrument and its tone is brightened by placing it near a fire.

It is noteworthy that the name each drum receives makes reference to the function it fulfills, in a manner quite like the later naming of the rumba *cajones*. The biggest drum bears the name *caja*, although is it also called *llamador* ("caller"). The mid- sized drum is called *mula* but also *segundo* and *dos y dos*. The smallest is called the *cachimbo* or sometimes *quinto*. The similarity to the names of the rumba *cajones* is self-evident.

Yuka Drums, Matanzas Province

To play, the musician remains seated with the drum between the legs and resting on the ground. The drumhead is struck with both hands using both palms and fingers. Occasionally, the drummer might strike the head with one or two sticks. The resulting cross-rhythms underlay the improvisations of a singer alternating with responses sung by a chorus. The music may serve a religious purpose for a ritual of the Palo Order, although it is also used for secular celebrations staged by people of Congo heritage.

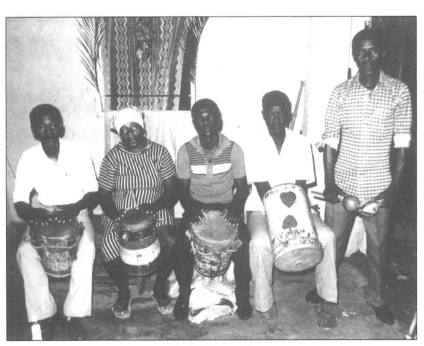

Kinfuiti Ensemble

The *ngoma* or *palo* drums are also used to accompany the *kinfuiti* drum. This practice, however, survives only in the village of Quiebra Hacha in the province of Havana.

The *makuta* drums, also brought to Cuba by Congo or Bantu people, are yet another forebear of the conga drums. These drums may have tubular, cylindrical, or barrel-shaped bodies. They each have a single head with the lower end open. The head is tensioned by the heat of a fire since the membrane is tacked onto the shell of the drum. Recently produced models are commonly tensioned with a more complex system of lugs and turnscrews.

Makuta festivals are ceremonial celebrations which originated and still exist in the societies of the Congo people and their descendants. They were very common during the 19th century and were still not infrequent during the early decades of the 20th century. In Cuba, the word *makuta* indicates a festive gathering. The term also refers to a kind of ritual staff to which is attached a spherical receptacle containing magical elements or objects. This staff or *makuta* is used at certain moments in the ceremony to strike the ground in a rhythmic accompaniment to a song or dance. According to believers, it houses the supernatural power on which are centered all of the activities of the Palo Order. However, the individual names of the drums—*caja, ngoma,* and *nsumbi*—make no allusion to those of the rumba *cajones.*

Makuta Drum Party, Trinidad, Sancti Spiritus

The shape of the drums' bodies and the system for tuning the *ngoma* and *makuta* drums provided the Congo people and their descendants with the construction elements needed for the conception of a drum such as the conga. Polyrhythms based on the combination of three different sized drums with well defined individual functions are likewise linked to the *tumbadora* by these African drums. Moreover the tacked head and the practice of brightening the tone with heat from a fire which characterized the early congas had their antecedents in the *ngoma* and *makuta* drums. The head played on directly with the hands may be linked to almost any drum of African origin, however, the nature of rumba's cross-rhythms and many details of the ways they are played remind us again of what we have heard on drums of Congo origin.

The observed practice with *ngoma* drums of striking with two sticks on the wooden shell of the instrument is surely the precursor of the two spoons striking the side of one of the rumba *cajones,* as earlier described. This practice was passed on to the congas and in rumba received the name of *cáscara.*

It is worthy of note that in the voluminous work, *Instruments of Afro-Cuban Music* by Fernando Ortiz, published in Havana in 1954, the term *tumbadora* does not appear. The expression *tumbador* appears as a term for "certain drums in rumba and conga orchestras" (Ortiz, F. 1954: IV - 168). In this same work, Ortiz indicates that one of the congas—conga drums—is given the name of *tumbadora.* Evidently, Ortiz is referring to congas since he himself later indicates that these instruments "have been introduced into orchestras and popular combos which today are styled for boleros, *guarachas,* mambos, etc." (Ortiz, F. 1954: IV - 168). There appears, however, an extensive article by Ortiz in the third volume of the aforementioned work under the title "The Conga" where it is evident that here the author is referring to Cuban *tumbadoras.*

Ortiz describes the word *conga* as "an African drum, but this word is also applied to a dance, a song, the music played, danced, or sung with this beat and to the street bands which use such instruments" (Ortiz, F. 1954: III - 392). When Ortiz describes the instruments he indicates that they are "drums made nearly always of staves with iron hoops, about a meter long, somewhat barrel-shaped, open with a single ox-hide head affixed with tacks. They are essentially heat-tuned drums which must be repeatedly re-tuned at the fire" (Ortiz, F. 1954: III - 392).

At first only two congas were played. The first was given the name *caja* or *mambisa* and the second was called *salidor* or *tumbador.* Ortiz himself states that only later was a third drum incorporated which was designated by the name *quinto.* He states also that the three drums are of approximately the same size, although he does not indicate that the difference in pitch of each relative to the other two is determined by the difference in head diameter of each drum.

It is remarkable that Ortiz should indicate in 1954 that "the term *conga* is of relatively modern introduction in Cuba" (Ortiz, F. 1954: III - 398). For him, it is only near the end of the 19th century that in Cuba's eastern region drums called congas were played in the carnival street bands. However, he also indicates later that "the conga was born in Havana in times of Spanish rule" (Ortiz, F. 1954: III - 400). He furthermore states that the purpose of the stave-built drum was to differentiate it from African drums—generally made from hollowed tree trunks—because of the prohibition to which they were subject. If we take into account all of Fernando Ortiz's aforementioned descriptions and assertions, we can conclude that the name *tumbadora* or conga to designate these drums is a phenomenon of the second half of the 20th century. We can further conclude that there was a certain connection between the instruments used for congas and carnival street bands and those used for the rumbas. It is fitting to mention that both musical streams originated in the marginalized and peripheral barrios of Havana and Matanzas and in the same segment of the populace.

It is significant that Ortiz asserts that "Nowadays special drums are not required for playing rumba. Rumba is a dance and a rhythm but not a drum," and goes on to say that the drums used for rumba are not historically related to the drums called *congas*, inasmuch as the fashionability of the latter has all but eliminated the former, and that in present-day popular dance bands when rumbas are played congas are used, creating a certain confusion since today many are unaware that there were special drums called *rumba drums* (Ortiz, F. 1954: IV - 104). From this we can infer that the advent of the conga in Cuban music is not an event remote in time. The earliest mention of the instrument dates from the first decades of the 20th century.

All of the available information suggests that the most primitive congas first appeared in carnival street bands. However, the rhythms and style elements that characterized their debut as musical instruments came from the rumba *cajones*. It is also in the rumba context that the conga reaches its definitive form and acquires the head tensioning system that it presently possesses. For this reason we prefer to place the birth of the conga in the context of rumba, and to see the drums of the carnival street bands as just one more predecessor of these instruments. The evolution of the old-time conga drums brought about the birth of another type of drum called *bokú*, which did develop into a form suitable for playing in the street marches which the carnival demands.

Some authors state, I think rightly, that during the third decade of the 20th century the first congas began to be introduced at rumba gatherings. This occasioned less frequent use of the *cajones* at such gatherings. Furthermore, each conga took over the job of one of the *cajones* so that there were three congas, each quite different in size and function. Each of the congas similarly took over the name of the *cajón* it had replaced.

The phonetic antecedent of the word *tumbadora* we find in the expression *tumba*, an Afro-American word denoting drums in general. Both words—*tumba* and *tumbadora*—contain the phoneme *mba* which is evidently of Bantu or semi-Bantu origin. This is one more clue leading us toward the large Bantu group of peoples in our search for the historical predecessors of the Cuban instrument.

In the 1930s the congas' use at rumba festivals became systematized. The instruments had the barrel shape obtained by stave construction—just as we see today—but the head was attached to the body of the drum. This was in urban areas of the provinces of Havana and Matanzas. This period was characterized by a strong migratory movement toward eastern Cuba, since the sugar industry was growing in that direction and, with it, the Cuban railway system. This offered job opportunities to many living in western Cuba, who moved eastward principally during the time of the sugar harvest. This internal migration shifted the conga into the eastern parts of the country. In fact, congas are found during that era in the remote mountain regions of Baracoa.

Perhaps it is worth noting that the spread of the conga's use throughout the country is not linked to the development of rumba. The rumba fiesta as such remained, with numerically insignificant exceptions, a western Cuban happening. The spread of the conga itself beyond the fiestas in which it originated was because the instrument outgrew its rumba setting to become part of very different Cuban musical groups and ensembles focused most often on playing *son*, bolero, and *guaracha*.

The *son*, a traditional music genre of rural eastern Cuba, had reached Havana during the 1920s and there taken on new forms of interpretation. Among the instruments that were quickly adopted for playing urban *son* music were the piano and the conga. Thus the conga became known among communities of people who had no connection with the rumba fiestas, and thereby it encountered more widely generalized forms of Cuban popular dance in that period.

From 1939 on, the famous dance orchestra Arcaño y Sus Maravillas included the conga permanently in its lineup. This lead was to be followed by other orchestras and by bands and combos playing the popular dance music of that time. Perhaps the first to make the conga part of his group and hence part of the so-called *Cuban conjunto* was the famous musician and composer Arsenio Rodriguez. From that time on the conga became a key voice for playing *son, guaracha,* and, later, bolero. The conga rapidly became fashionable and was included in ensembles and typical groups throughout nearly all of the country.

Studies carried out by the Center for the Study and Development of Cuban Music reveal that the orchestra "Renovación de Jiguaní" in what is now Granma Province was using a stave-built and tacked-head conga as early as 1942. Elsewhere these studies reveal that in 1940, a band in the village of Ensenada de Cortés in Pinar del Río was already using its first conga.

The culmination of the conga's rise in popular Cuban dance music of the 1940s was when it outgrew its national boundaries. In 1947, Dizzy Gillespie's famous jazz band engaged the outstanding percussionist Chano Pozo as the band's conga player. This was a crossroad for American jazz and brought about the rise of a new stream now known as Afro-Cuban jazz.

In that era the conga still had its tacked-on head, but its international triumph in the field of jazz necessitated improvements over the unreliable skin tensioning system. Thence came the complicated tensioning system with its metal head rim, hooked screws, and tensioning lugs, ensuring that the instrument did not gradually slip out of tune during extended periods of performance. It also made it possible to tune the head far higher than ever before, greatly brightening the drum's sound.

By the 1950s, the new tuning system was widespread and was even in use by many rumba ensembles in Cuba. The famous rumba group "Los Muñequitos de Matanzas" was by 1954 playing congas with the new tuning system when it burst onto Cuba's music scene, mainly via radio programs heard throughout the country. In the 1970s, the conga with its new tuning system was showing up in the most diverse groups in international music, especially North American music. By then, the conga possessed all the required qualities to take its place among musical instruments of acknowledged international stature. Its tuning system enabled it to play with instruments requiring tempered tuning. Its repertoire thus included nearly all of Cuba's musical genres and it was easily adapted to many other popular music genres throughout the Caribbean and Latin America. Important also was the fact that it had been taken into the mainstream of American jazz, which in turn served as a bridge to the rock and pop music of today.

Modern Tuning System

Since the rise in the mid 1950s of the nationalist movement in Cuban concert music the conga has been heard as an instrument of the symphony orchestra. But in the 1970s, the instrument also began to appear in the writing of non-Cuban composers. Some important Cuban concert music works in which the conga appears are: *Rítmicas IV and VI* for Cuban percussion instruments and *La Rebambaramba,* an African ballet, both by Amadeo Roldán; *Three Cuban Dances* for symphony orchestra and the opera *Manita en el Suelo* by Alejandro García Caturla; *Music Alive no. 1* for percussion instruments by José Loyola; and *Yagruma* for symphony orchestra by Carlos Fariñas. In the 1980s and 1990s the conga became more of a presence on the international music scene, not only because of the strong growth of Cuban music on that scene but also because nowadays it appears ever more frequently in a wide range of international pop music settings.

Modern Cuban Tumbadoras

Notation Key

In this book, music is notated on a two-line staff. Here are the notehead symbols and articulations that indicate the different kinds of tones.

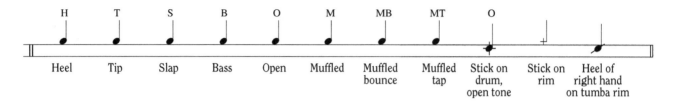

The drum to be played is indicated by the placement of the notehead.

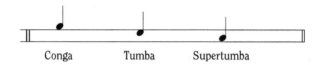

The hand to use when playing a drum is indicated below the staff: "L" for the left hand, "R" for the right hand.

Conga Basics

The Names of the Drums

Each drum in the "conga family" has many names. Here's what Poncho calls each drum.

Conga, Tumba, Supertumba

Poncho plays this way, with the *tumba* to the right and the *supertumba* further down. Once in a while Poncho plays *quinto* (smallest "conga" drum) on the left, but he can get most of the *quinto* sounds right from the conga.

The Sounds of the Drums

TRACK 2

There are four main tones you'll want from the congas. They are the bass tone, the open tone, the muffled tone, and the slap. You should be able to get these sounds with either your right or left hand.

The Bass Tone

The Bass Tone

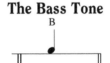

Use the palm of your hand to get the bass tone. You should be able to play the bass tone with either hand.

The hand should remain relatively flat on the drumhead; strike down on the middle of the head with the flat of your hand.

Tuning Your Drums

Patato—Carlos Valdés—showed me how to tune the drums. He was one of the first guys to use two congas. Most Cuban cats used one drum; you know, the old style. Patato plays so melodically. When he came to New York, he began using up to five drums. When I heard him play using just three drums, I had to ask him how he tuned—he sounded so different than Mongo. I found out that Patato played *tres*, the Cuban guitar that is comprised of six strings divided into three pairs, so he tuned his conga like a C chord. It fits in with the harmony of a lot of the songs in my band—it doesn't go against the harmony at all. So, I tune the conga to C, the *tumba* to G, and the *supertumba* to E.

—*Poncho Sanchez*

The Open Tone

You should be able to get a good open tone with either hand.

The Open Tone—Left Hand

The Open Tone—Right Hand

Poncho raises his left hand off the conga, leaving the wrist on the rim of the drum, while the right hand plays the open sound. The striking hand should be held loosely with the fingers spread. The part of the hand where the fingers join it should strike near the rim of the drum; the fingers should make contact with the drum head (but should still be near the edge of the drum).

The Muffled Tone

Right Hand Open Tone with Left Hand Resting

Muffling on the Edge of the Drum

It's just as it sounds—it isn't an open or a slap tone. You can muffle the drum in the center of the drum or on the drum's edge as shown.

The fingers should be held together, and the hand flat. Achieve the muffled sound by pressing down on the head and not releasing immediately. You can strike near the edge of the drum or the middle, but whatever you do, make sure you muffle the tone with the other hand.

The Slap, *Tapao*, or Pop

The slap is a very important part of playing congas. You need to develop the open as well as closed and mini slap sounds. Note that all of the slaps are notated in the same way—it is up to you to decide which to use, based on the musical context. Poncho uses the open

The Slap

slap primarily in soloing, the closed slap is used for both soloing and the actual grooves, and the mini slap is used only in *chachachá* or in slower tunes such as the "Guajiras."

Poncho deadens the head with his other hand while playing a slap, depending on the type of sound that is being played. In the picture on the previous page, you can see Poncho's right hand playing a slap, with the left hand deadening the sound of the drum.

The open slap tone can be generated with either hand, but make sure your other hand is entirely off the drumhead. Cup your fingers, bend your thumb out of the way (you don't want it to make contact with the drum) and strike the edge of the drum sharply—the last three fingers should feel a "sting." You can also play this tone closer to the middle of the drumhead.

When Poncho plays the closed slap sound, one hand is in the center of the drum, muting it. He then cups his other hand and strikes the drum, just as in the open tone.

The Mini Slap

With the mini slap, both hands are on the drum. The mini slap is played as part of the overall groove, and is typically played with the non-dominant hand. This hand should be in "playing position," with the heel of the palm near the drum edge, and the sound is generated by a quick snap down of the last three fingers of this hand. Poncho creates the mini slap sound with the left hand.

A muffled bounce—which is notated the same as a muffled tone, but with an "MB" instead of just an "M"—is a sound that comes directly out of a slap. After the slap, this is the resultant bounce, much like a "ghost note" after an accented snare hit. Your hands should be in the same position as for a slap, but the fingers should be held more loosely, even though the muffled bounce is played with the same hand.

The muffled tap—notated the same as a muffled tone, but with an "MT" instead of just an "M"—is simply a soft tap that usually occurs after a closed or open slap.

The Tilting of the Conga

Poncho naturally tilts the conga when he plays. I find it's the comfortable way for me to play, too. Also, tilting the drum opens up its sound. Poncho tilts the conga towards the *tumba*—this makes it easier to get to the *tumba* when he plays a two-drum pattern. Some others tilt the drum in different ways, but most players at least like to have the bottom of the conga off the floor.

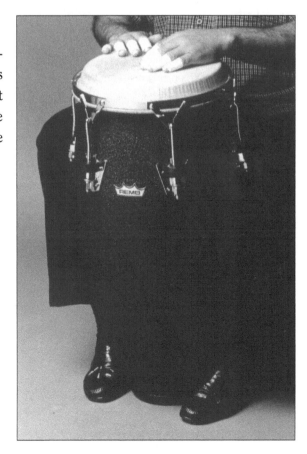

Important First Motions on the Conga

These four motions are ones that you will want to master. The heel-tip and slap motions are essential to playing the congas.

Heel

Tip

Slap

Tip

For the heel movement, rest your hand, palm down, on the drum and strike with the heel of the palm on the edge of the drum. For the tip movement, again rest your hand on the drum, palm down, and strike the drumhead with the tips of the fingers.

REFRIED BEANS AND SPANISH RICE

Beans

1/2 cup lard
Salt and pepper
2 15-oz. cans pinto beans
1/4 cup Monterey Jack cheese, shredded

Place the lard in a frying pan. Heat the lard to a liquid state over a medium to high heat, and continue to keep it very hot. Add a bit each of salt and pepper to taste. Drain and set aside the water from the cans of beans. Place the beans in the frying pan with the lard—be careful, as the lard may splatter! Cook the beans for approximately ten minutes. Add some of the reserved bean liquid if the beans look dry. Keeping the pan over heat, mash the beans with a hand potato masher and then blend in the Monterey Jack cheese.

Rice

1/4 cup vegetable or canola oil (*not* olive oil)
Salt and pepper
1 cup uncooked, long grain, white rice
1 small tomato, diced
1/2 medium-sized onion, diced
4-5 cloves garlic
2 cups water
1 15-oz. can chicken broth
1 8-oz. can tomato sauce
Oregano to taste

Heat the oil over a high heat in a deep frying pan. Add salt and pepper to taste, plus the rice, tomato, onion, and garlic. Cook for eight minutes. When the rice turns brown, the vegetables are cooked. Add the water, chicken broth, tomato sauce, and oregano. Add additional salt and pepper to taste and stir. As soon as the mixture comes to a boil, lower the heat to medium and cover. Cook for 20 minutes. Let stand for ten minutes. Serve with refried beans.

Chachachá

Preliminary Exercises for *Chachachá*

Throughout the *Conga Cookbook* you will find preliminary exercises. The goals of these exercises are:

1. To help you to acquire specific techniques to help you groove.
2. To help you to learn the distinct parts within these techniques.
3. To help you to find the "real groove."

The preliminary exercises are short phrases which should be practiced slowly and with a focus on good sound coming from proper technique. This will help you to develop the sound and feel of the grooves found in each section of the book.

In these preliminary exercises, and throughout the *Conga Cookbook* and Afro-Cuban music in general, you will find *flams*. A flam is a way of "thickening" a beat by adding a slightly softer stroke right before a main stroke. This softer stroke is called a *grace note*. Poncho creates flams with either hand and in two different ways: very open (with the two notes spread apart) and more closed (with the grace note and main note struck almost simultaneously). Mostly, Poncho plays flams with the right hand playing the grace note and his left hand playing the main, stronger note.

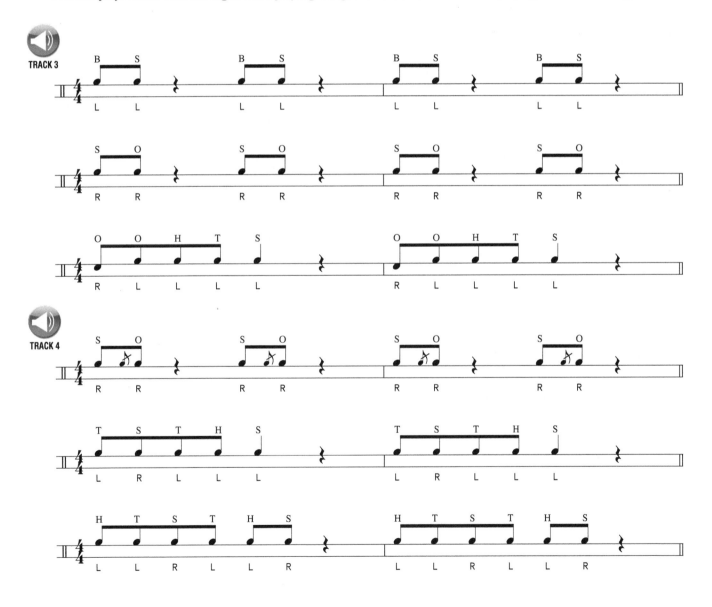

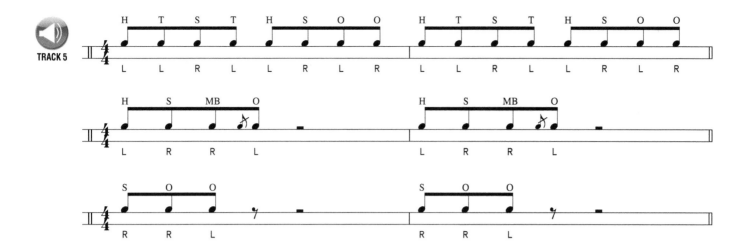

Mongo Santamaria—Our First Meeting

Mongo Santamaria is one of my friends. The first time I met Mongo was at the Lighthouse in Hermosa Beach, California. I was in high school; I used to ask cats in my neighborhood in Norwalk for rides to the beach. It was a long way, so I gave them 50 cents for gas—hey, it was a couple of gallons back then! I was a big fan of Mongo when he played with Cal Tjader. The Lighthouse would let me and my friends in for half price with student IDs. We'd sit in the kid's section. We were in a big nightclub sitting on the side, each drinking our soda with a cherry in it, and here's Mongo. I mean, he was why I was there—Cal's band had Mongo and Armando Peraza in it. We'd show up an hour early and I'd sit and stare at all of those drums on stage. The first time I went I brought a record and Mongo signed it. When he walked on stage and started playing, I was in heaven!

—*Poncho Sanchez*

Mongo Santamaria and Poncho, July 1988

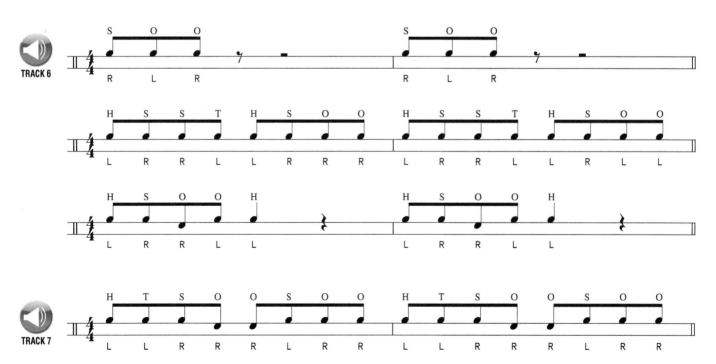

20

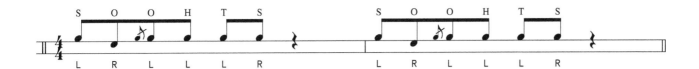

Basic *Chachachá*—"Two-point Shuffle"

Poncho uses this basic conga groove when playing *chachachá*—he calls it the "two-point shuffle."

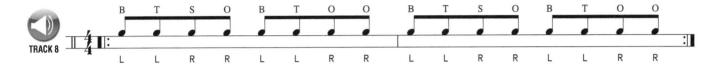

There are many variations that Poncho uses for the *chachachá*. Some use two drums: the conga and the *tumba*. *Chachachá* was first played only on the conga, but over the years the *tumba* has been added, especially in the Latin jazz context.

By the way, here's your chance to practice the mini slap. Poncho got this "little slap" before the one open tone from Mongo Santamaria—he would do it in the slower tunes like the "Guajiras." This slap is played by the left hand, within the groove itself.

Patterns for *Chachachá*

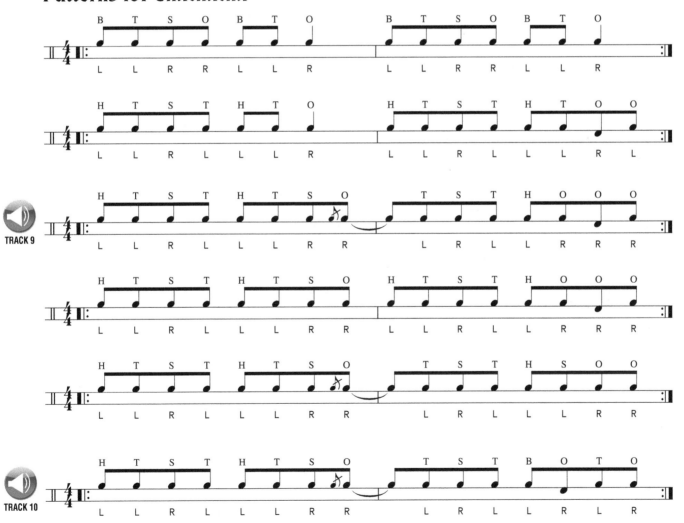

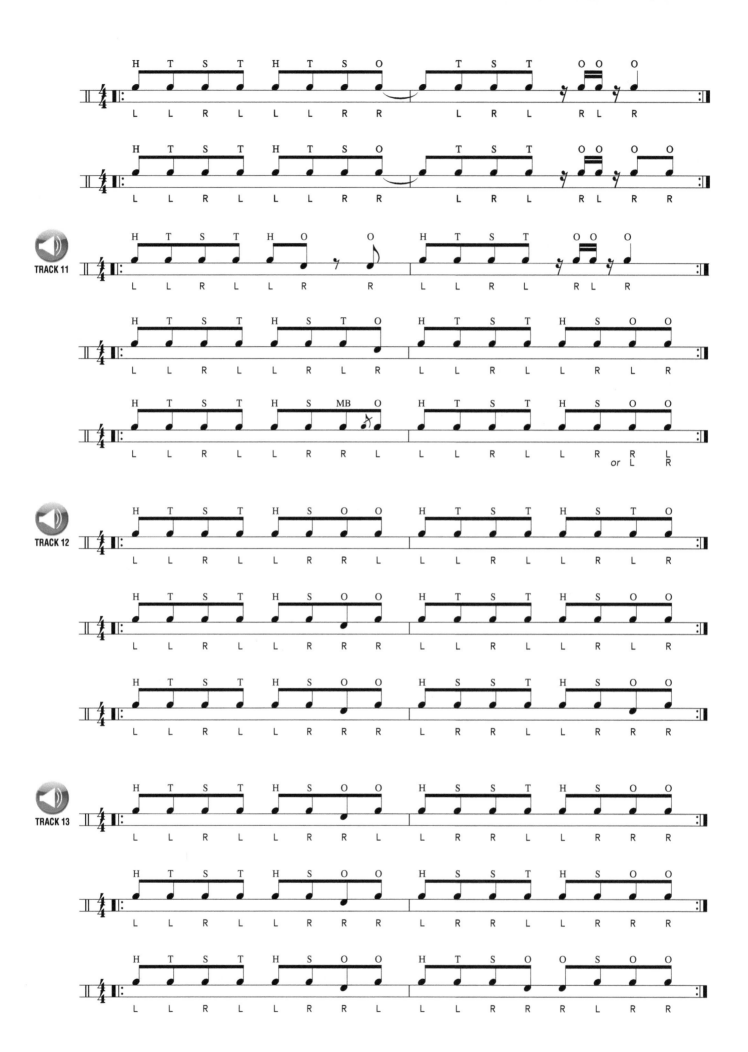

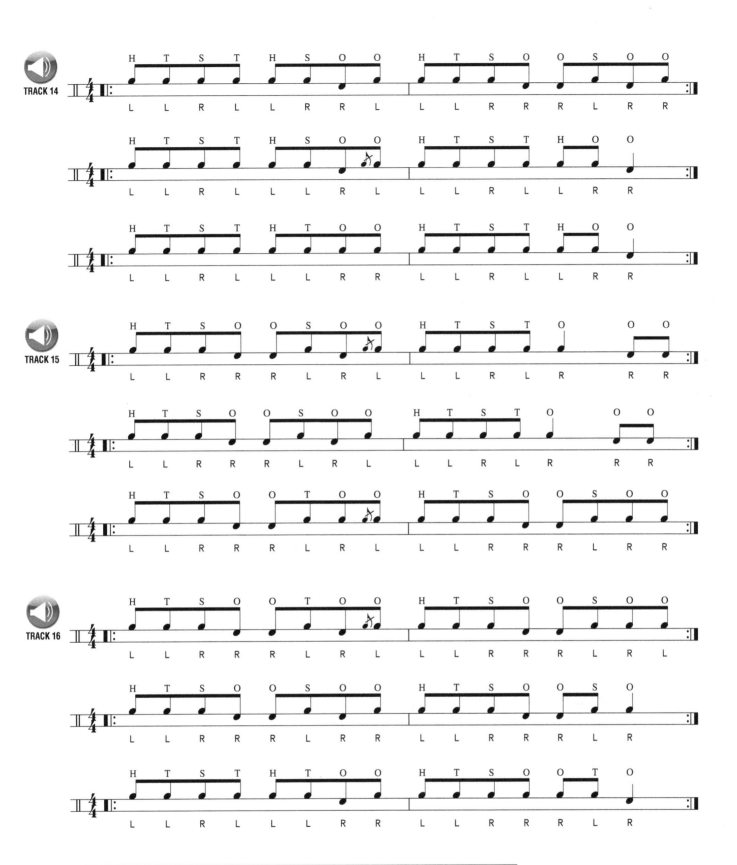

Kids

I try to help kids when I can. When my band goes to a city, we visit a university or school there. I do a workshop with the bands, giving them advice—"do this," "don't do that." We play tunes together—we all have fun and learn from each other.

—*Poncho Sanchez*

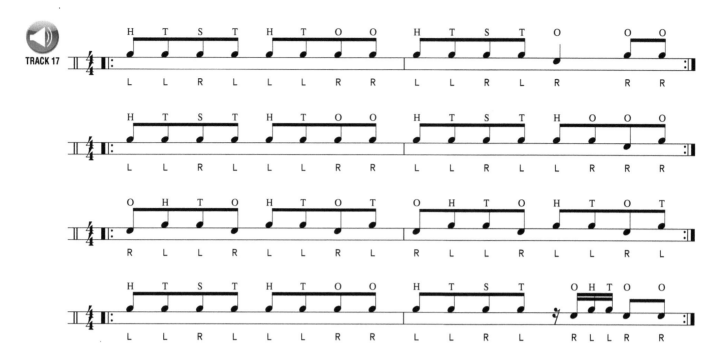

Chachachá Play-along

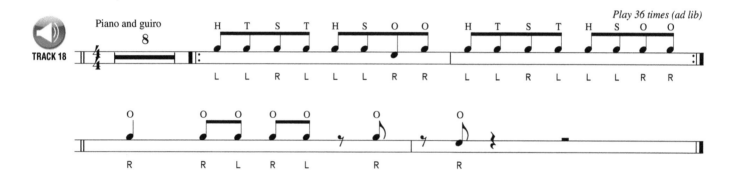

CHICKEN, CORN, AND CALABASITA (ZUCCHINI)

1/4 cup vegetable oil

Salt and pepper

2 1/2 cups cubed chicken

1 medium tomato, diced

1/2 small onion, diced

4-8 cloves garlic

4 zucchinis, sliced 1/2" thick

4 ears fresh corn on the cob, shredded from the cobs

1/2 cup fresh cilantro

1 cup water

1 8-oz. can tomato sauce

1 15-oz. can chicken broth

Crushed red chile and/or diced jalapeño to taste (optional)

Heat a large skillet and add the oil. Add salt and pepper to taste and throw in with the meat. Cook until the meat is browned, about ten to 20 minutes. Add the tomato, onion, and garlic and cook for eight minutes. Add the zucchini, corn, and cilantro and cook for an additional five to eight minutes. Add the water, tomato sauce, and chicken broth, plus the red chile or jalapeño to taste. Bring the mixture to a boil and cook for 20 minutes. Let stand for ten minutes before serving.

Mambo

When Poncho plays mambo and moderate- to up-tempo Latin jazz, he uses the three-point shuffle. Poncho also uses the common two-drum *marcha* most of the time, different from the one-drum pattern that he plays, in *chachachá*. *Marcha* is a common term used by conga players, and refers to the "march" groove we most often associate with the sound of the congas.

There are many variations in this mambo section. Here are some exercises to get you used to the hand movements. Refer to the Notation Key if you have a problem with the sounds of the drums.

Preliminary Exercises for Mambo

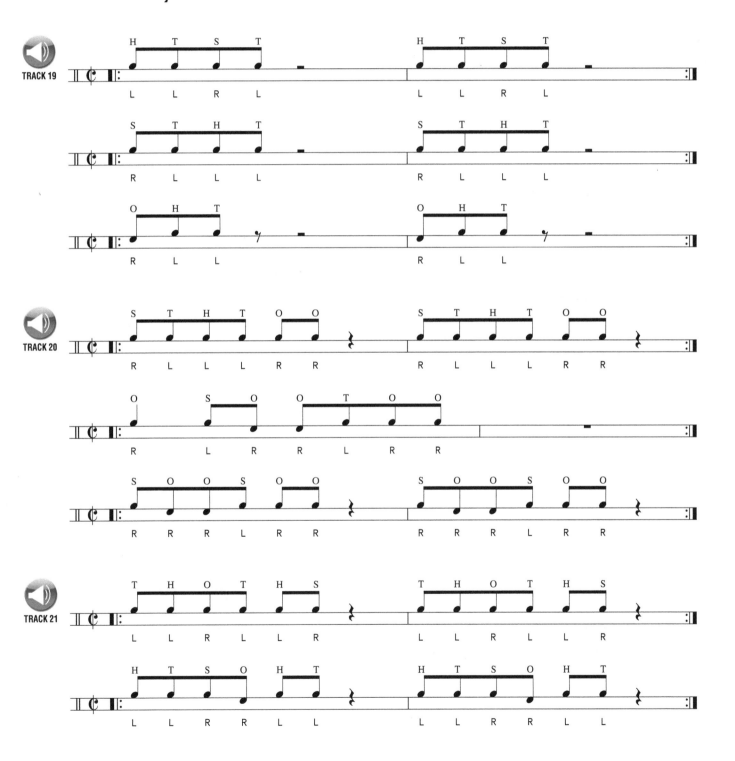

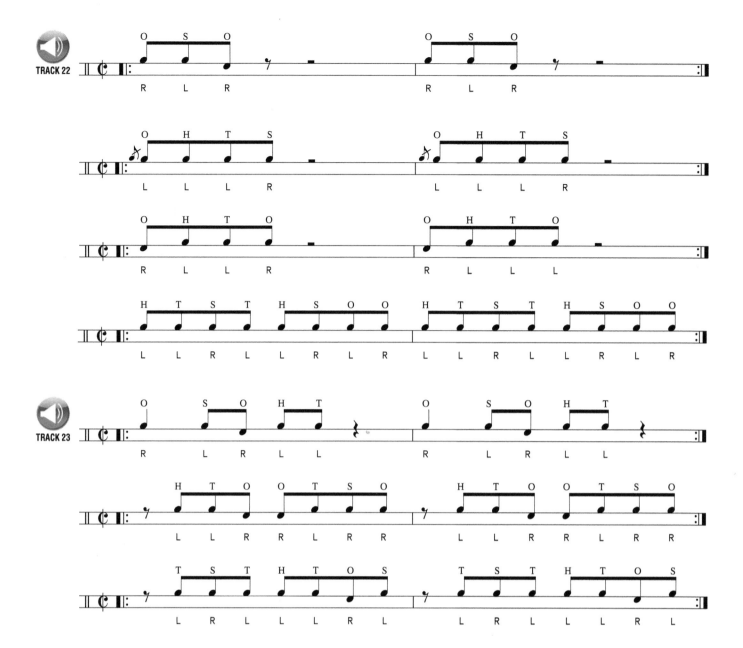

Mongo and My Son

As I got older and Mongo saw me at all of Cal's Los Angeles gigs, Mongo and I became good friends. After I got married, my wife Stella and I would go and hear Mongo together. Once, when Stella was pregnant, we went to The Pasta House in East L.A. to hear Mongo play. We asked him to touch Stella's stomach for good luck, and I told Mongo that if the baby was a boy we would name it after him. Well, Xavier Mongo Sanchez is my son. Every time Mongo and I see each other, he still asks, "How's the boy? How's Monguito?"

—*Poncho Sanchez*

Basic Mambo—"Three-point Shuffle"

TRACK 24

Flams are used in these grooves also, as well as in the *chachachá* and soloing. Sometimes Poncho follows a flam with a stroke in either hand, and sometimes he just lets one note go by. In either case, the groove has to be respected—it's what the dancers feel. Flams are used to thicken the groove and add taste and flavor. You can think of the notes here as not being very close together, but more spread apart in order to produce a thicker tone.

Patterns for Mambo

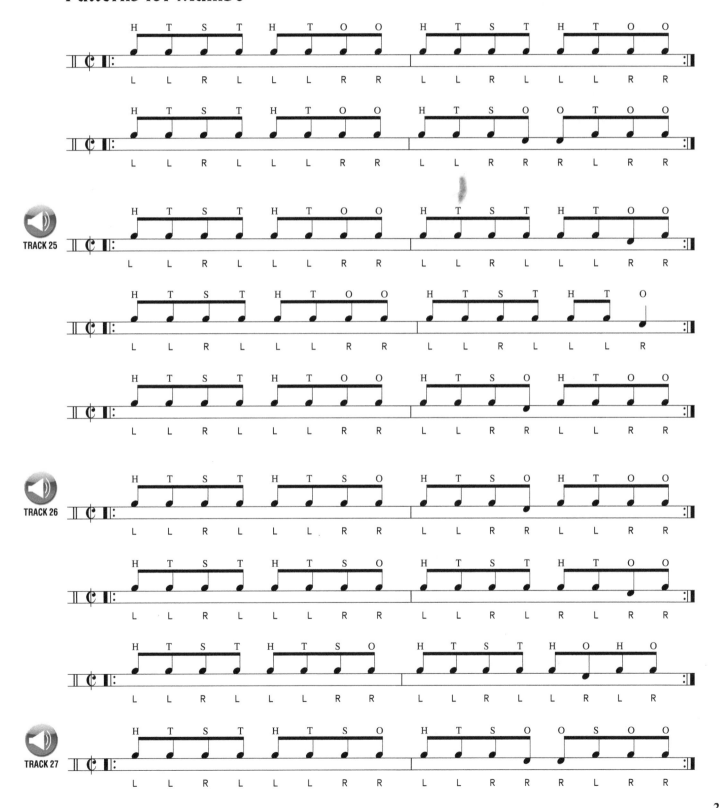

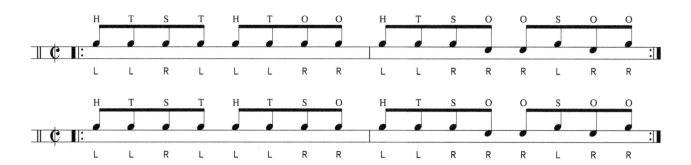

Latin Drums All Over

Nowadays, you find Latin drums in all types of music. Congas, timbales, bongos, guiro, and maracas have found their way into all styles. It's good for us as musicians, and good for everybody!

—*Poncho Sanchez*

Poncho with the University of Southern California Marching Band

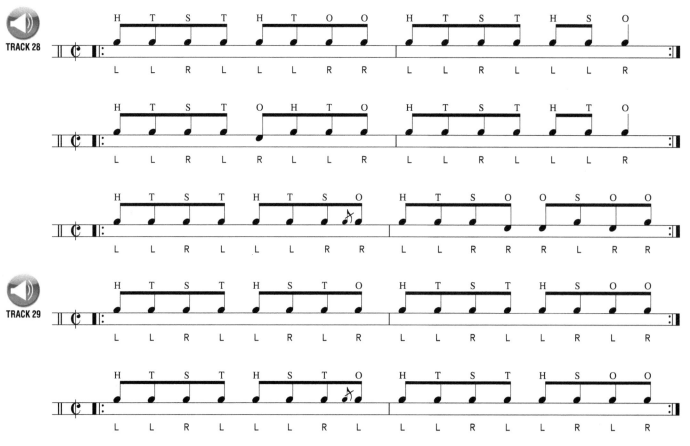

TRACK 28

TRACK 29

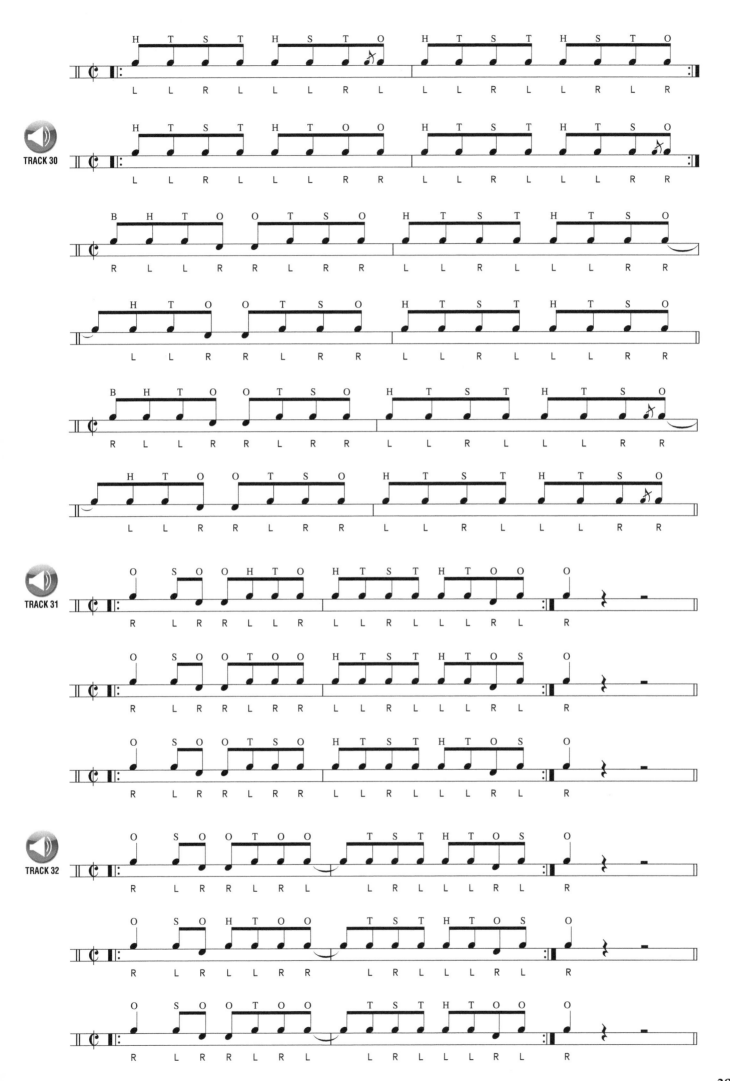

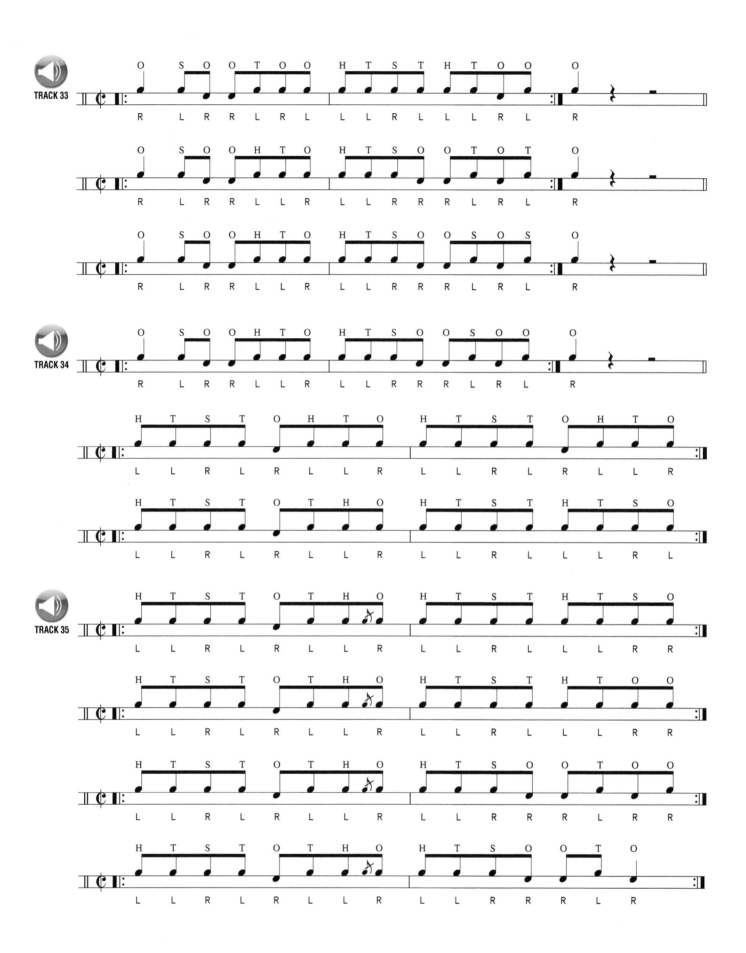

Clare Fisher—A Real Class Act

When I first joined the Cal Tjader band, Lonnie Hewitt was playing keyboards. Two years later, Clare Fischer joined the band. I had heard of Clare because of songs he had written such as "Pensativa" and "Morning." I was impressed. He's very health conscious and he's brilliant—a harmonic genius. He speaks perfect Spanish—he used to correct me because I'm "from the neighborhood." He was in Cal's band in the 1960s, and then left for 16 years. At first, we were bumping heads a little—I'm from the barrio and he's not. He'd be adding these augmented jazz chords and I'd be asking him to play more *típico*—it's a "fine line" because we were both playing Latin jazz. Finally, we hit upon a happy medium, and then Clare and I started our own band, Salsa Picante. Just from being around him every other day, I learned a great deal—I really studied with Clare. I heard some beautiful melodies and harmonies that ended up inspiring me when it was my time to do my own albums. We recorded four albums together with Salsa Picante—we even won a Grammy together. Through five years together, I really grew musically, but Clare and I had differences of opinion. One day, Clare said, "You know Poncho, I think it's time you get your own band." After he told me that, I drove home, not feeling so good. I told my wife Stella how upset I was, and she told me, "Poncho, maybe Clare's right!" I sat down for a while and realized that they were *both* right—and look what happened!

—*Poncho Sanchez*

Mambo Play-along

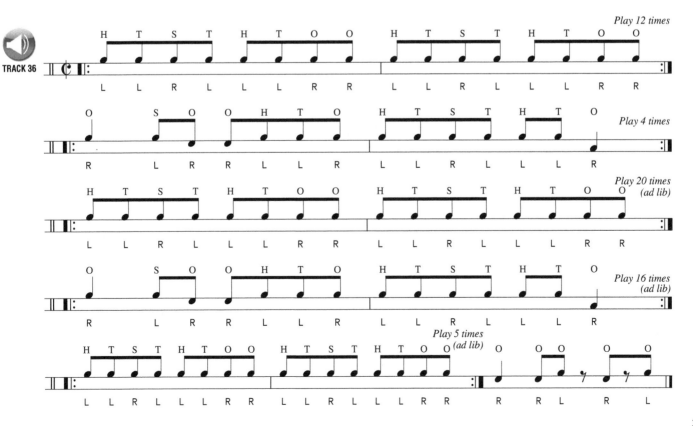

31

CHILE CON SOUL

1/4 cup vegetable oil

Salt and pepper

4 medium-sized pork chops (include bones for flavor)

1 medium yellow onion, sliced

2 4-oz. cans Ortega Green Chiles, diced (or 8 whole New Mexico green chiles)

4 cloves garlic

1 28-oz. can of whole peeled tomatoes, squished by hand

1/4-1/2 cup red, dried, crushed chile (to taste)

1 cup water

1 8-oz. can tomato sauce

Heat a large skillet and add the oil. Add the pork chops and then salt and pepper to taste; brown for ten minutes. Add the onion, green chiles, and garlic. Cook for four minutes. Add peeled tomatoes, chile, water, and tomato sauce. Cover and simmer for 20 minutes. Let stand for ten minutes and serve.

6/8 Rhythms

The rhythms of 6/8 that Poncho plays come from Africa and Cuba. These rhythms are deep and moving, and they affect people in ways that Poncho sees every night when he performs. He learned how to play 6/8 rhythms from watching and listening to great *congueros* like Mongo, Patato, and many others.

Once again, you'll find some standard patterns here and then variations on themes. The important thing to strive for in this and the other sections of the *Conga Cookbook* is a deep groove with a warm, inviting sound coming from your drums.

Preliminary Exercises for 6/8

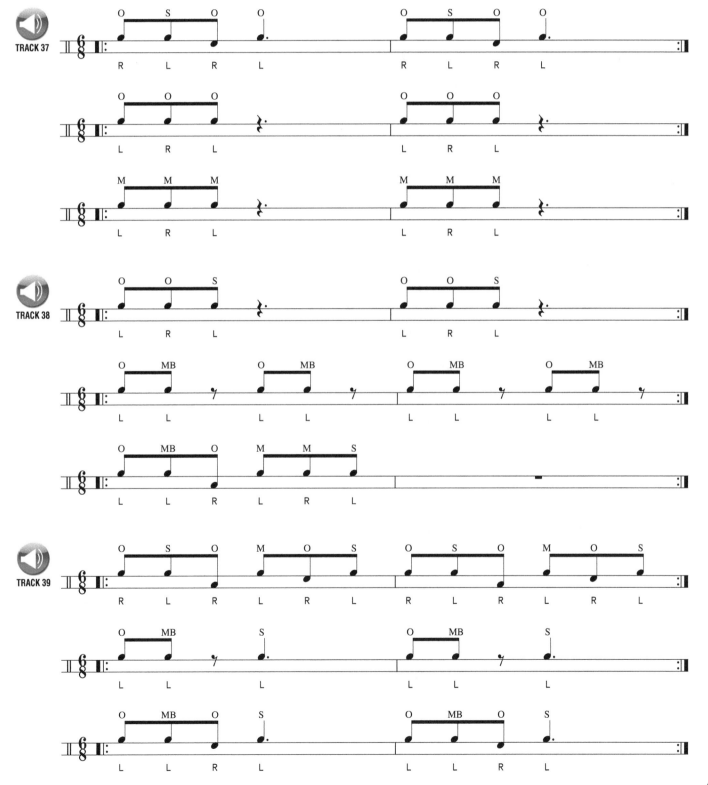

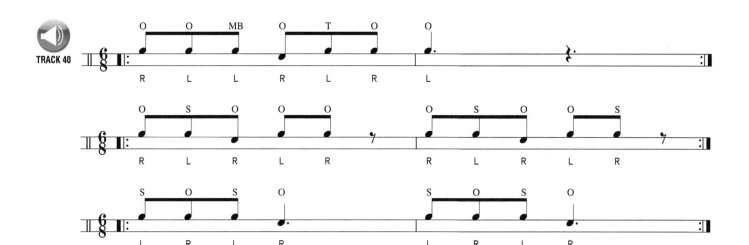

A Big Surprise!

When I first joined Cal Tjader's Band in 1975, we were playing in San Francisco opposite Tito Puente's band. Mongo Santamaria was the guest with *both* bands—so now he wasn't signing my records anymore! I was playing with Cal on a very high stage and all of a sudden I felt someone grab my leg—it was Mongo! After the set, we met backstage. He told me that I had his old job and that "hey man, you're sounding good!"

—*Poncho Sanchez*

Basic 6/8

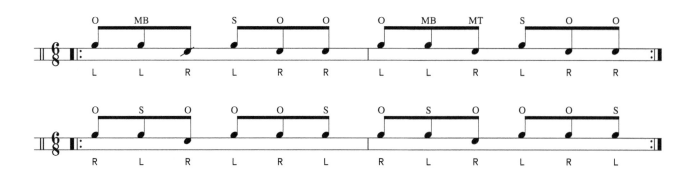

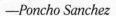

Patterns for 6/8

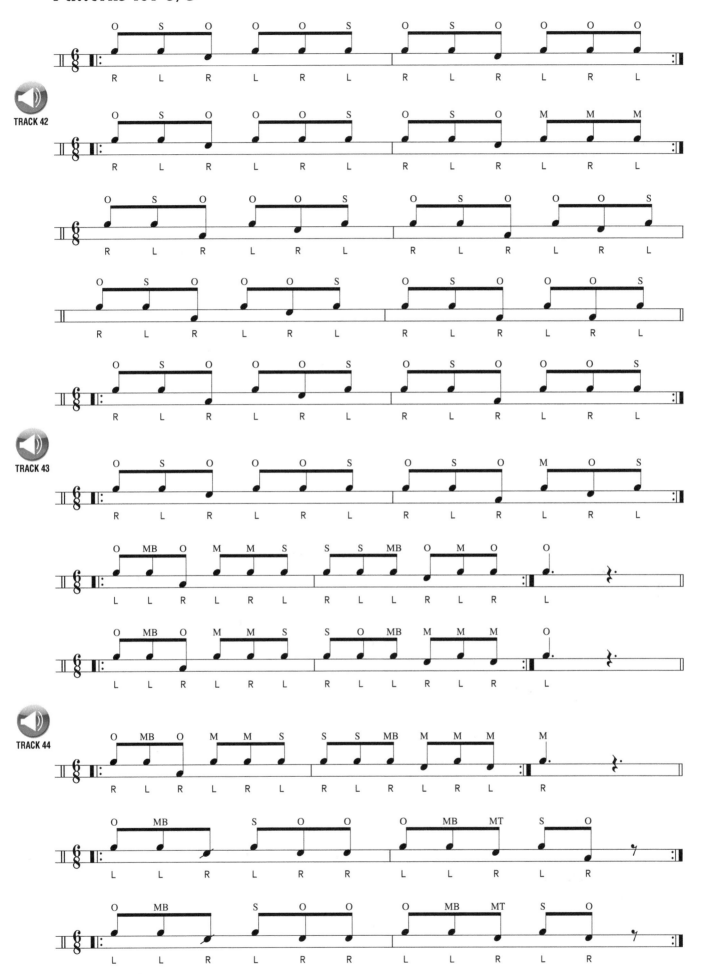

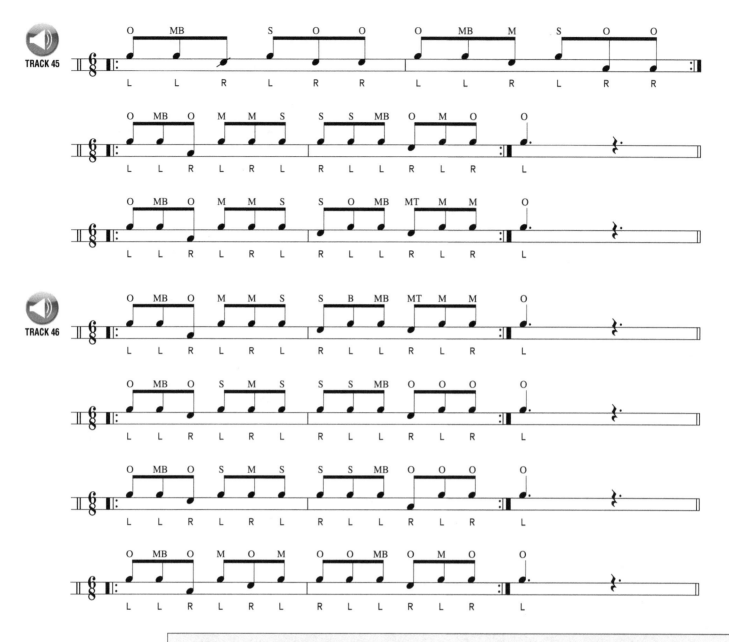

Our Second Trip to New York City

We were taking a cab ride to The Village Gate—Monday night, Salsa Meets Jazz. Man, we saw this big, long line all the way down Bleecker Street. I asked the cabby what the line was for—I thought it was for a movie or something. We got to the front of the club and there was the marquee, saying "Tonight Only—Poncho Sanchez Band." We almost died! And who was there that night? Tito, Manny, Patato, Kako … all of our favorite guys.

—*Poncho Sanchez*

6/8 Play-along

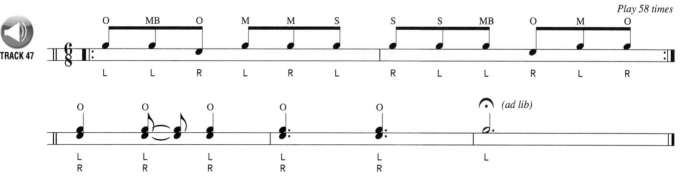

LINGUINE WITH CLAM SAUCE

Clam Sauce

Extra virgin olive oil (enough to cover 1/4" in frying pan)

Salt and pepper

10 cloves garlic, diced

1/2 cup fresh parsley, chopped

6 6-oz. cans chopped clams

1 cup white wine

1 28-oz. can whole peeled tomatoes

1 8-oz. bottle clam juice

Open all cans before you begin. Squish the tomatoes by hand, drain, and reserve juice. Drain the juice from the canned clams and reserve. Heat a frying pan over high heat, and then add enough oil to cover 1/4" of pan. Add salt and pepper to taste, plus the garlic and parsley. When the garlic turns golden brown, add the clams and mix well. Add the white wine and cook for two minutes, allowing the alcohol to burn off. Add the tomatoes and clam juice. Simmer for 15-20 minutes.

Linguine

1/4 cup olive oil

1 1-lb. package linguine

1 pat butter

Pinch of salt

Cook the linguine according to the directions supplied with the pasta, but before adding the linguine to the pot of boiling water, add to the water the olive oil, butter, and salt. When the pasta is al dente, drain but do not rinse with cold water. Serve with clam sauce.

Merengue

Merengue is a rhythm from the Dominican Republic. There are many ways to play *merengue*—shown here are the ways Poncho plays this dance rhythm. Poncho really has one basic pattern that he uses. It may vary a little, depending on the dancers.

In order to play these patterns, you'll need a stick to play the rims and heads of your drums. Hold the stick loosely in your dominant hand—there is really no further technique to holding the stick, but you want to hold it tight enough so that you can strike the rim or head, but not so tight so that the sound is choked. For the open tone, strike the open drumhead as you would any other drum; for the rim sound, strike the rim as you would any other drum rim.

Poncho plays *merengue* on *tumba*, and when he plays the *apanbichao* (double-time feel for *merengue*), Poncho adds the *supertumba*. Of course, you can use one or two drums if you wish.

The sound of the left hand on the *tumba* is more like a half open and half slap. Poncho uses the left hand to keep time and fill in.

Apanbichao

When the music really starts to get hot, Poncho's rhythm section goes into this groove—it's like a doubling up of the tempo. Depending on how crazy and funky he wants to get, Poncho adds certain other sounds.

There's a line between 4/4 and 6/8—you can see it and feel it with the dancers—so the triplets in these patterns are not really "pure" triplets. They fall somewhere in between the two time feels. It's hard to transcribe this notation, so listen to the recording to get a good feel for it.

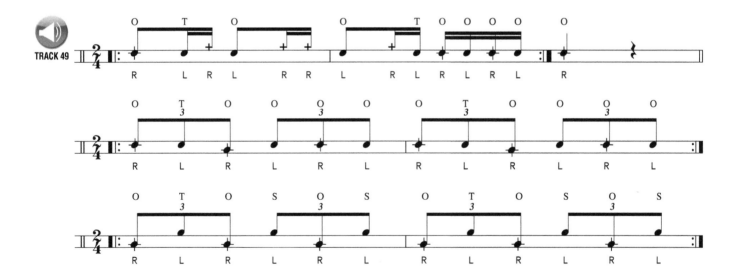

Manny Oquendo is Boss!!

Timbalero Ramon Banda plays hard—and Manny plays hard, too. Ramon found these bolts for holding the bells on the *timbales*—heavy-duty stuff. He gave Manny a batch of them when we went to New York. He saw them and the first thing he said was, "Aww, these are 'boss'!" I mean, that's the way he talks. What I dig about Manny so much is that he plays solid and real hard. He's right there every time—real *típico*. He doesn't play real fast but he plays with authority and a lot of strength—real funky sounding, loose *timbales*. That's where I've gotten a lot of my *timbale* stuff. In the early days he was with Eddie Palmieri's band La Perfecta—he played bongos, bell, and *timbales*.

—*Poncho Sanchez*

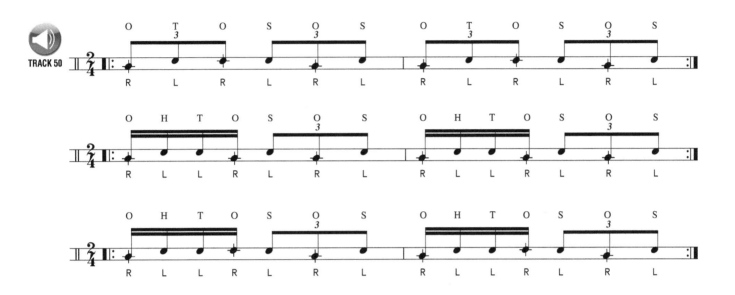

Merengue Play-along

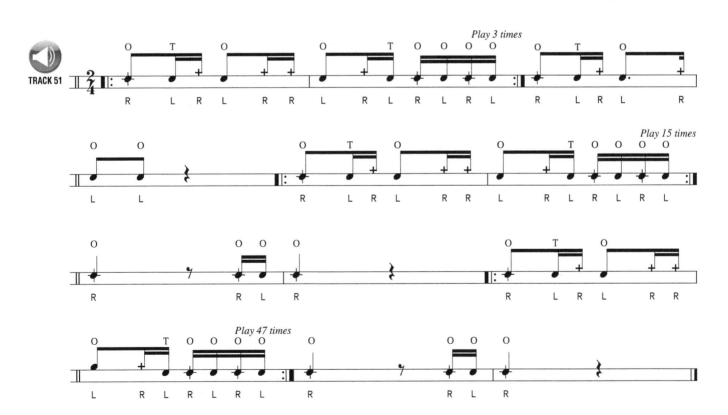

POSOLE

Salt and pepper

4 lbs. lean pork butt, cut into 1" dice (20 chunks)

1 beef foot, quartered

1 whole yellow onion, skinned

Bay leaves

Oregano

2-3 28-oz. cans hominy

1 28-oz. can Las Palmas Red Chile Sauce

Fill a deep soup pot half full with water and bring to a boil. Add salt and pepper to taste, plus the pork butt, beef foot, whole onion, several bay leaves (to taste), and oregano (to taste). Cook for one to two hours at a medium flame, or until the meat is thoroughly cooked. Add the hominy and chile. Cook for an additional 15 minutes and serve.

Soloing

Soloing on congas is an art form which, in order for a player to develop, involves listening to the greats and their solo styles, taking the time to develop your technique, and then developing your own styles using both feel and technique.

Presented here are two solos played by Poncho. The first solo is in a *chachachá* groove, the second solo is in a mambo groove. Before the second piece, you'll find exercises to play to ready yourself for the full version.

You will find within the solos a method of phrasing that Poncho and other *congueros* use. The heel-tip motion is used extensively as a timekeeping movement, but also to keep the groove alive. These warm-up exercises below will help you to loosen up and to develop the heel-tip motion.

Warm-up Exercises

I developed these exercises to help you to get the heel-tip motion together. Some of the exercises are straightforward and some require you to use your counting skills, as they involve odd note groupings such as fives and sevens. I suggest the use of a metronome to help you to develop a good sense of time.

This first exercise involves 16th notes and 32nd notes. Take it at a slow tempo and strive for a feeling of a relaxed flow in your wrists.

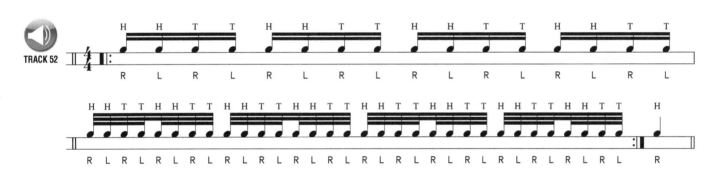

This exercise involves an interesting use of the slap-heel-tip motion. You can use the open stroke instead of the slap, or alternate the motions to get different sounds. Moving the open or slap movement to different drums will also open up your ears to different possibilities. Note that here you'll be playing sextuplets. Watch the motion of your hands and strive for relaxed motion and good sound.

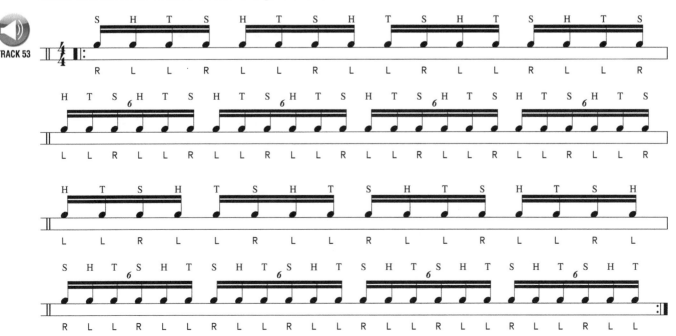

These next two exercises use odd note groupings to help you to develop the heel-tip motion. You can develop the motions effectively by beginning them on different parts of the beat—the odd groupings of five and seven notes help you to do just that. The use of a metronome here is advised, as you'll want to make sure that you're playing the correct number of notes per beat.

This exercise involves the playing of 16th notes for one measure, followed by a measure of quintuplets. Maintain the heel-tip motion throughout the quintuplets; do this by splitting the heel-tip motion in two (between the first and second quintuplets and between the third and fourth quintuplets).

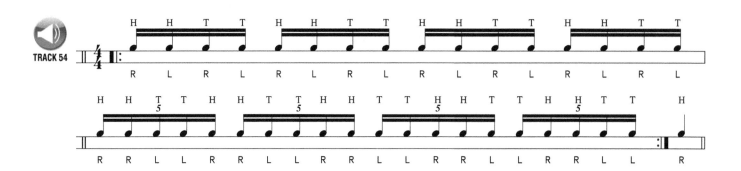

This exercise involves the playing of 16th notes for one measure, followed by a measure of septuplets. Maintain the heel-tip motion throughout the septuplets; do this by splitting the heel-tip motion in two (between the first and second septuplets and between the third and fourth septuplets).

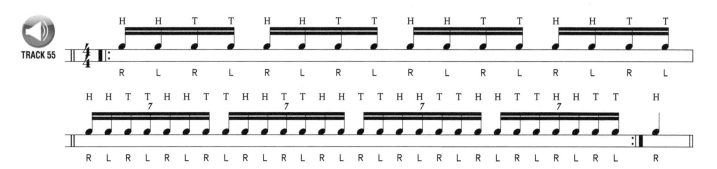

Solo #1

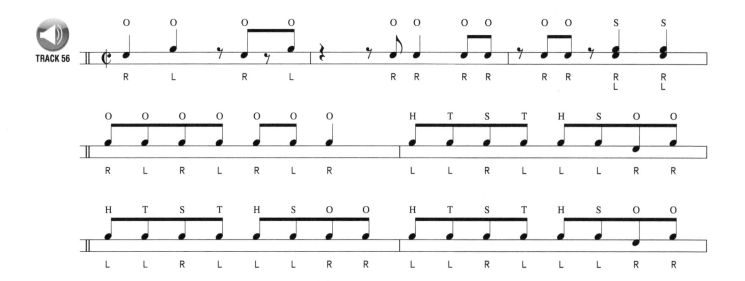

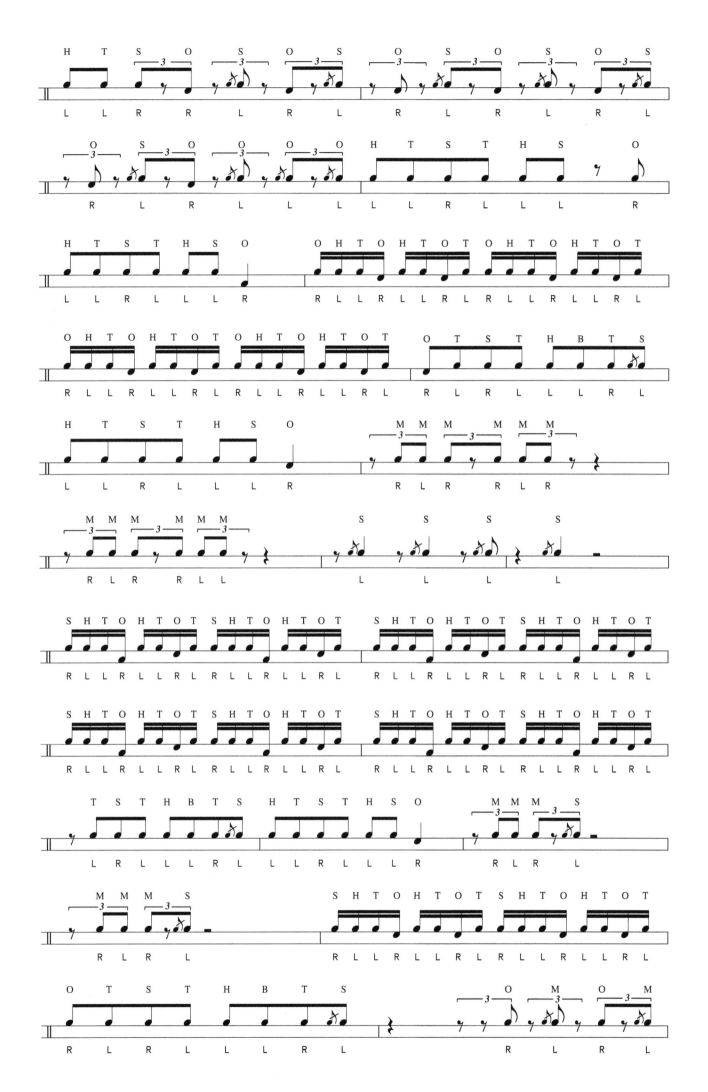

Patato and My Hat

I was playing with Cal at the Irvine Bowl in Irvine, California. Patato was playing with the Tito Puente Band. I had been with Cal for three years before I met Patato. At that time, I was just tuning my drums the way I liked. I asked Patato how he tuned his drums, and he sat right down at my drums and tuned them. That's when I learned about the C-E-G tuning. Well, we started talking. I was wearing a white hat just like Patato—I told him I'd seen pictures of Patato wearing the hat, and he said he'd been wearing this style of hat for years. He asked to see my hat and told me I hadn't been wearing it right. He motioned for me to follow him—to the men's room, right into a stall. What's going on here? He started pulling toilet paper off the roll and putting it into the sides of the hat, to help it hold its shape. It was my first lesson with Patato, and it was how to tune my drums—and how to wear my hat!

—*Poncho Sanchez*

Preliminary Exercises for Solo #2

These phrases represent some very important methods of phrasing that may come in handy when you tackle Solo #2. Notice that even though you may not actually hear some of the strokes, they are there. Listen to the solo to hear and feel the *sabor* ("flavor"). Then, try to play the preliminary exercises first before going on to the solo.

Here, as well as in other solo phrases, you will find the heel-tip motion as a timekeeping and ghost note device.

Poncho plays two very fast taps with left tip in the first four 16th notes of this phrase. They're almost like two fast double strokes.

This is an interesting phrase, using alternating single strokes beginning with the left hand.

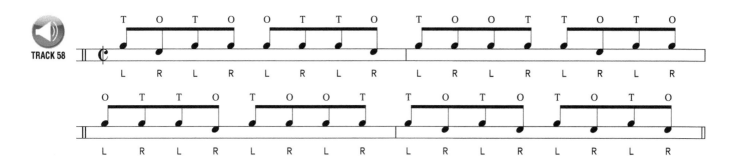

A very rapid heel-tip motion is featured in this phrase.

Even though you may hear only the open tones, the heel-tip articulation is here, too!

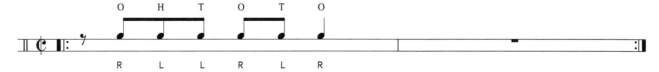

Once again, the heel-tip articulations are used for timekeeping and as ghost notes.

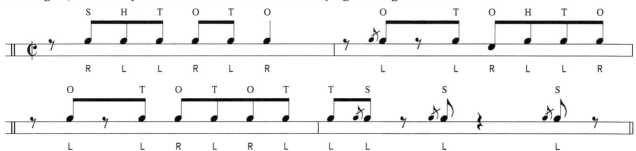

These are phrases where taking your time to work through the issues will really pay off. The heel-tip motion is used in three different ways: in triplet, eighth note, and 16th note phrasings. This all demonstrates how this motion is utilized throughout this and many solos, as well as many other ways of playing.

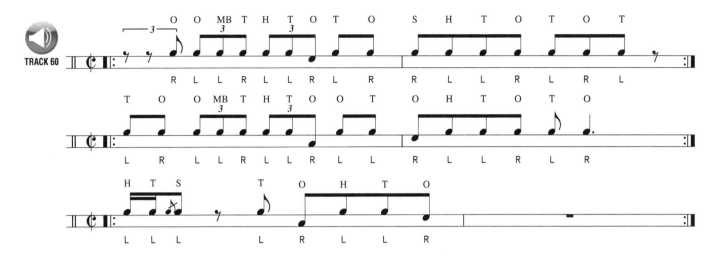

Here's a great phrase that allows you to work on your slaps!

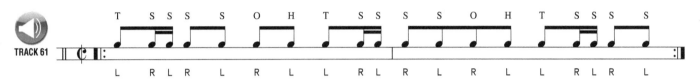

Here, the slap, heel-tip, and open sounds are used to create an elegant phrase.

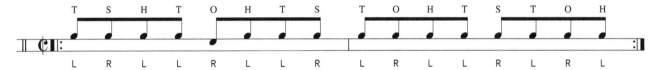

El Maestro Tito Puente

Tito and I were partners—our bands played so many gigs together all over the United States, we couldn't help but become close. He'll always be "The Maestro." I used to listen to Tito's records when I was growing up in Los Angeles. Every time Tito came to town, I'd go and hear him. I really studied his playing. Eventually we became very good friends. I must have played a hundred times with Tito.

—*Poncho Sanchez*

Solo #2

Listen to Solo #2 before you try to play it in its entirety.

TRACK 62

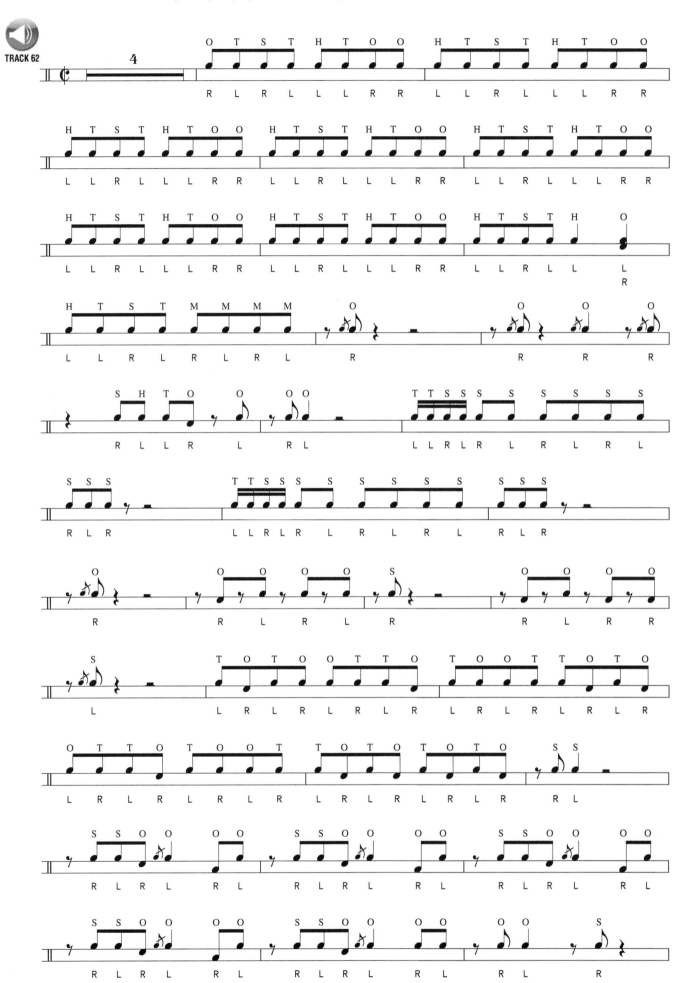

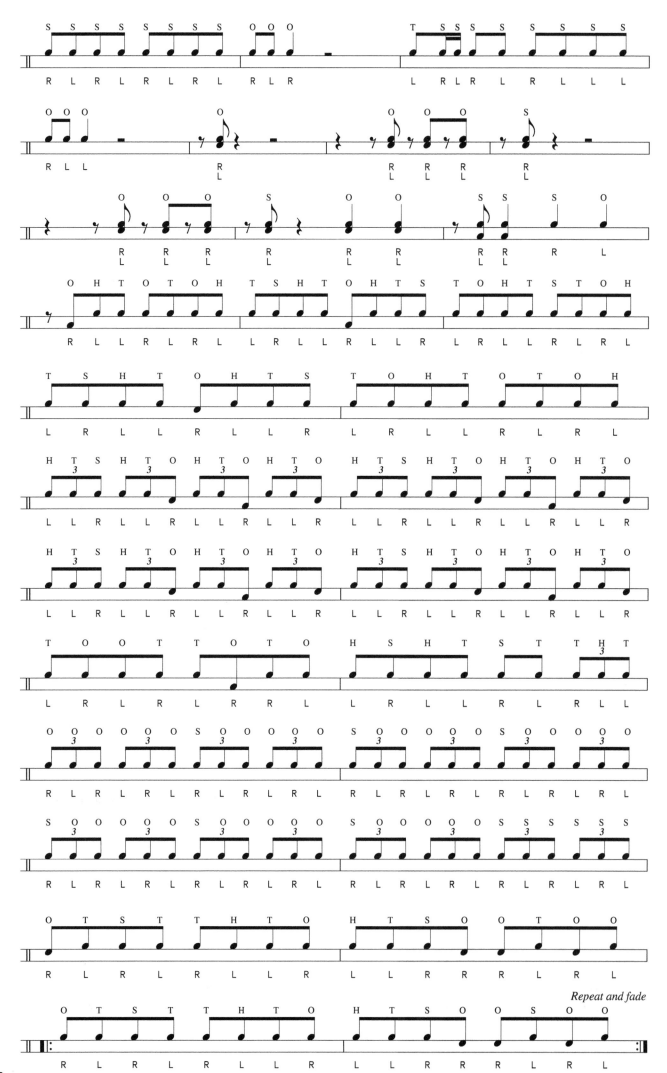

ALBONDIGAS (MEAT BALL SOUP)

1 1/2 gallons water

3 tbs. Knorr Suira Chicken Flavor Bouillon

2 lbs. lean hamburger meat

1 tsp. salt

1 tsp. pepper

1 tsp. garlic salt

1/2 cup onion, diced

1 medium tomato, diced

3 cloves fresh garlic, diced

1 cup fresh cilantro, chopped

1/2 cup all-purpose flour

1 cup long grain rice

2 eggs

1 stick celery, 1" slices

1 carrot, 1" slices

2 medium zucchinis, 1" slices

1 8-oz. can tomato sauce

1 tsp. oregano

Fill a deep pot with the water and add two tablespoons of Knorr Suira Chicken Flavor Bouillon. Bring to a boil and cook for 20 minutes. While the bouillon is boiling, prepare the meatballs.

Place the meat in a large mixing bowl and add the salt, pepper, garlic salt, one tablespoon of chicken bouillon, onions, tomato, garlic, cilantro, flour, 1/2 cup of rice, and eggs. Hand mix all ingredients. Make eight to ten medium-sized meatballs, using all of the mixture.

Add the meatballs and then the vegetables to the simmering bouillon. Add the tomato sauce and 1/2 cup of rice. Bring to a boil and add salt and pepper to taste. Lower the heat to medium, cover, and let cook for 45 minutes. Serve with corn tortillas.

Recommended Recordings

Here are some great CDs from which you can learn so much about this music. Poncho has spent hundreds of hours with these maestros, and he hopes you'll find a lot of *sabor* here, too!

Tito Puente: *Top Percussion/Dance Mania* (RCA Victor, #BCD 15687)
Tito Puente: *Puente in Percussion* (Tico, #TRLP-1011)
Both of these recordings were experimental at the time—no one had ever recorded these kinds of percussion albums before. You can clearly hear Tito, Mongo, Willie, and Patato playing very authentic patterns and rhythms. This is the way you want your drums to sound.

Cachao: *Cachao y su Ritmo Caliente from Havana to New York* (Caney, #CCD 501)
Listen to Tata Guines' great sound and solo ideas.

Candido: *Brujerias de Candido* (Tico, #TSLP 1142)
Listen to Candido's solo on the track "Take More Candi." I learned a lot from this solo, including how to phrase my solo ideas.

Cal Tjader: *Monterey Concerts* (Prestige, #PCD-24026-2)
Listen to the great bongo solo on the track "Tu Crees Que"—powerful slaps! On the track "Tumbao," listen to Mongo's great solo ideas, especially how he goes from 4/4 to 6/8.

Cal Tjader: *Soul Burst* (Verve, #V6-8637)
Listen to Patato's great sound and melodic playing.

Cal Tjader: *Soul Sauce* (Verve, #V6-8614)
Listen to Armando Peraza's great sound and style of playing.

Mongo Santamaria: *Our Man In Havana* (Fantasy, #FCD-24729-2)
This album contains the sound of the son, conjunto, guaguanco, rumba, *batá,* and charanga.

Mongo Santamaria: *Afro Roots* (Prestige, #PCD-24018-2)
This album contains the sound of the son, guaguanco, rumba, and batá. *I learned how to solo on a* chachachá *(two-point shuffle) by listening to the track "Mazacote."*

Tito Rodriguez: *Big Band Latino* (Palladium Records, #PCD-117)
Listen to the track "Esta Es Mi Orquesta"—this is a music lesson in itself.

Tito Rodriguez: *The Best of Tito Rodriguez & His Orchestra Volume 1* (RCA, #3419-2-RL)
Here's more great Tito Rodriguez music to practice with and listen to.

Ray Barretto: *Indestructible* (Fania, #LPS 00456)
Listen how the band plays very tightly and together.

Ray Barretto: *Carnaval* (Fantasy, #FCD-24713-2)
This album contains the charanga *and* conjunto *sounds, and also includes Chombo Silva on saxophone. Listen for Ray Barretto's crisp and clean playing.*

Willie Bobo: *Uno Dos Tres 1, 2, 3* (Verve, #V6-8631)
Listen for Victor Pantoja's clean and crisp sound.

Eddie Palmieri: *Sentido* (MP, #MPPK-5-6251)
Eddie Palmieri: *The History of Eddie Palmieri* (vocals by Ismael Quintana) (Tico, #TSLP 1403)
Both of these are great records to practice with.

Joe Cuba Sextet: *Diggin' the Most* (Seeco, #SCCD-9259)
This is the first recording I learned to play with.

Papin y Sus Rumberos: *Guaguanco Conjunto Guaguanco Matancero* (Antilla, #CD-565)
Patato: *Patato y Totico* (Mediterrano, #MCD-10065)
Both of these records have great rumba and guaguanco *playing and singing.*

MORE HOT DRUM BOOKS AND DVDs FROM CHERRY LANE

STEVEN ADLER'S DVD VIDEO
GETTING STARTED WITH ROCK DRUMMING
Taught by the Legendary Former Guns N' Roses Drummer!

02501387 DVD.........................$19.99

AFRO-CARIBBEAN DRUM GROOVES
by Chuck Silverman
02500370 Book/CD Pack.........................$14.99

THE BOOK OF FUNK BEATS
Grooves for Snare, Bass, and Hi-hat
by David Lewitt
02500953 Book/CD Pack.........................$14.99

PONCHO SANCHEZ' CONGA COOKBOOK
by Poncho Sanchez with Chuck Silverman

02500278 Book/CD Pack.........................$16.95

DOUBLE BASS DRUMMING AND POWER FILLS WORKOUT
by Matt Sorum and Sam Aliano
02501670 Book.........................$14.99

DRUM EXERCISES FOR THE POP, FUNK, AND R&B PLAYER
by Ralph Johnson
02500827 Book/CD Pack.........................$14.99

DRUMMING THE EASY WAY!
The Beginner's Guide to Playing Drums for Students and Teachers
by Tom Hapke
02500876 Book/CD Pack.........................$19.95
02500191 Book Only.........................$12.95

DRUMMING THE EASY WAY! VOLUME 2
by Tom Hapke
02501064 Book.........................$12.95

LATIN FUNK CONNECTION DVD VIDEO
taught by Chuck Silverman
02501417 DVD.........................$16.99

BEST OF THE DAVE MATTHEWS BAND FOR DRUMS

02500184 Play-It-Like-It-Is Drum.........................$19.95

DAVE MATTHEWS BAND – FAN FAVORITES FOR DRUMS
02500643 Play-It-Like-It-Is Drum.........................$19.95

METALLICA – ...AND JUSTICE FOR ALL
02503504 Play-It-Like-It-Is Drum.........................$18.95

METALLICA – BLACK
02503509 Play-It-Like-It-Is Drum.........................$18.95

METALLICA – DRUM LEGENDARY LICKS
taught by Gregory Beyer
02500172 Book/CD Pack.........................$19.95

METALLICA – DRUM LEGENDARY LICKS 1983-1988 DVD VIDEO
A Step-by-Step Breakdown of Metallica's Drum Grooves and Fills
featuring Nathan Kilen
02500482 DVD.........................$16.99

METALLICA – DRUM LEGENDARY LICKS 1988-1997 DVD VIDEO
A Step-by-Step Breakdown of Metallica's Drum Grooves and Fills
featuring Nathan Kilen
02500485 DVD.........................$16.99

METALLICA – GARAGE INC.
02500077 Play-It-Like-It-Is Drum.........................$18.95

LEARN TO PLAY DRUMS WITH METALLICA
by Greg Beyer

02500190 Book/CD Pack.........................$14.95

LEARN TO PLAY DRUMS WITH METALLICA – VOLUME 2
by Dan Gross
02500887 Book/CD Pack.........................$15.95

METALLICA – MASTER OF PUPPETS
02503502 Play-It-Like-It-Is Drum.........................$18.95

METALLICA – RIDE THE LIGHTNING
02503507 Play-It-Like-It-Is Drum.........................$17.95

MODERN DRUM SET STICKINGS
by Swiss Chris
02501361 Book/CD Pack.........................$14.99

PONCHO SANCHEZ DVD VIDEO
Fundamentals of Latin Music for the Rhythm Section
featuring the Poncho Sanchez Latin Jazz Band
02500729 DVD.........................$24.95

1001 DRUM GROOVES
The Complete Resource for Every Drummer
by Steve Mansfield
02500337 Book.........................$12.95

66 DRUM SOLOS FOR THE MODERN DRUMMER
by Tom Hapke

02500319 Book/CD Pack.........................$16.99

RUSH – LEGENDARY LICKS FOR DRUMS DVD VIDEO
Taught and Performed by Jamie Borden

02500628 DVD.........................$24.95

See your local music retailer or contact:

cherry lane
music company

EXCLUSIVELY DISTRIBUTED BY
HAL•LEONARD® CORPORATION
7777 W. BLUEMOUND RD. P.O. BOX 13819 MILWAUKEE, WI 53213

Prices, contents, and availability subject
to change without notice.

1215

EXCEPTIONAL DJEMBES
from **tycoon®**
PERCUSSION

SIGNATURE HERITAGE SERIES DJEMBE

Constructed of hand-selected aged Siam Oak wood, this djembe features a brushed chrome Classic Pro hoop, reinforced side plates with 5/16" diameter tuning lugs, and backing plates. A single steel band surrounds the bottom of the bowl, providing added durability. The 22" tall drum has a dark brown matte finish, and a 12" diameter head made of hand-picked premium quality goat skin. A tuning wrench is included.
00755173 12"..$429.00

SIGNATURE PEARL SERIES DJEMBE

Constructed of eco-friendly and tonally superior Siam Oak wood, this djembe features a brushed chrome Classic Pro hoop, reinforced side plates and 5/16" diameter tuning lugs. It is 22" tall with a hand-picked premium quality goat skin head. A tuning wrench is included.

00755175 12"...$429.00

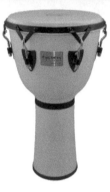

CANARY BURST KEY-TUNED DJEMBE

This is Tycoon's first ever key-tuned djembe! Constru... of hand-selected aged Siam Wood that provides excepti... durability and unmatched so... It features black powder co... Classic-Pro hoops, reinfor... side plates and large 5/... diameter tuning lugs. Equip... with a hand-picked prem... quality goat skin head. Tu... wrench included.

00142631 14"...$35...

MASTER HAND-CRAFTED ORIGINAL SERIES DJEMBE

As the name suggests, this drum is hand-carved by highly-skilled craftsmen, resulting in their unique and beautiful appearance. No two drums will look exactly the same! Constructed of hand-selected, aged Siam Oak wood, the djembe has exceptional quality and unmatched sound. It features a brushed Chrome Deluxe hoop, reinforced side plates with 5/16" diameter tuning lugs, and backing plates. The djembe is 22" tall, with a 12" diameter head made of hand-picked premium quality goat skin. A tuning wrench is included.
00755170 12"..$369.00

MASTER TERRA COTTA SERIES DJEMBE

Exceptional durability and unmatched sound come from this djembe constructed of hand-selected, aged Siam Oak wood. It features a Chrome Deluxe hoop, reinforced side plates with 5/16" diameter tuning lugs, and backing plates. Numerous layers of super high-gloss are applied and polished to create an attractive mirror-like exterior coat. The djembe is 22" tall, with a 12" diameter head made of hand-picked premium quality goat skin. A tuning wrench is included.
00755729 12"..$319.00

SUPREMO SERIES MAHOGANY FINISH DJEMBE

Constructed of hand-selec... aged Siam Oak wood, ... djembe features a black pow... coated Deluxe hoop, reinfo... side plates with 5/16" diam... tuning lugs, and backing pl... It is 22" tall, with a 12" diam... head made of hand-pic... premium quality goat skin... tuning wrench is included.

00755149 12"...$18...

TRADITIONAL SERIES AFRICAN DJEMBE

These traditional African Djembes feature shells hand-carved in Ghana from a single piece of hardwood. Premium quality unbleached goatskin heads provide for superior tonal qualities. 5mm non-stretch rope allows for easy and long lasting tuning.
00755188 12"..$239.00
00755187 10"..$199.00

Price and availability subject to change without notice.
For more details and other outstanding djembes, please visit
www.halleonard.com or **www.tycoonpercussion.com**.

FIBERGLASS ROPE TUNED DJEMBE

This djembe features a tonally superior shell, offering deep, loud bass tones and high, sharp slap tones. The extra strong non-stretch rope provides easy and long-lasting tuning.
00146173 12"..$95.00
00146172 10"..$79.00

RED MARBLE ROPE TUNED DJEMBE

This djembe features an eco-friendly and tonally supe... Mango Wood shell found in Northern Thailand. Each dru... outfited with a distinct handcrafted finish. Features deep, ... bass tones and high, sharp slap tones. 5mm extra strong r... stretch rope for easy and lasting tuning.
00142633 12"..$15...
00142632 10"..$11...

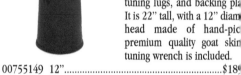
1

EXCEPTIONAL CAJONS

from **tycoon®**
PERCUSSION

SUPREMO SERIES HARDWOOD CAJON

The 29 Series Hardwood Box Cajon is constructed of durable and excellent sounding hardwood with a spruce playing surface. It yields deep bass tones and sharp high slaps, with fully adjustable snares. Each cajon is individually handmade and tested to ensure superior sound quality.

50307 ....$99.00

SUPREMO SELECT DARK IRIS SERIES CAJON

Individually hand-made and tested to ensure superior sound quality, this cajon features a Dark Iris body. It has adjustable snare wires and includes an Allen wrench.

42593 ....$129.00

CRATE CAJON
29cm

The body of this cajon is constructed of environmentally-friendly Siam oak, with exotic Asian hardwood and Siam oak front plates delivering superb tonal qualities. The hand-carved markings and wooden slats lined across the sides provide a distinct look and feel. Each cajon is individually hand-made and tested to ensure superior sound quality such as deep, d bass tones and high, sharp slap tones. Includes a snare usting Allen wrench.

755730 ....$174.00

PRACTICE CAJON

This cajon is designed for the player to practice and play with their favorite tracks. Just plug an MP3 player in the input jack and play along to the music! The front plate and body is constructed of environmentally-friendly Siam oak, and the cajon is easily transportable. It's powered by one 9V battery, and the snare wires are adjustable with the included Allen wrench.

00755234 ....$185.00

29 SERIES BUBINGA CAJON – MAKAH BURL FRONT PLATE

Individually hand-made and tested to ensure superior sound quality, this cajon has a Bubinga body and a Makah Burl front plate. Includes a snare-adjusting Allen wrench.

00755227 ....$199.00

35 ROUNDBACK SERIES CAJON – NORTH AMERICAN ASH FRONT PLATE

This special cajon features a curved back panel which provides for superior bass tones. The adjustable snares allow players to tune their cajon with the included allen wrench. The North American ash front panel provides enhanced acoustic tonal qualities.

13.75" x 20.5" front plate.
00755241 ....$249.00

VERTEX SERIES CAJON – AMERICAN ASH BODY AND ZEBRANO FRONT PLATE

This innovative cajon combines the sharp slaps of a 29 series cajon with the rich bass tones of a 35 series cajon. The unique pyramid shape is designed for improved ergonomics and comfort, and the body is American ash with a Zebrano front plate. There is an enhanced "sweet spot" for added resonance on deep bass tones. Includes snare-adjusting Allen wrench.

00755244 ....$259.00

32 SERIES DOHC CAJON

This unique cajon contains two separate chambers and sound holes, providing a versatile combination of deep, traditional bass sounds and crisp, tight, snare slaps. The body and front plate are constructed of environmentally-friendly Siam oak wood, and four rubber feet offer added stability when playing.

00755257 ....$299.00

TRIPLE-PLAY CAJON

A first of its kind, an all-in-one cajon designed to produce a great variation of cajon styles and sounds together in one drum features three distinctive playing surfaces each producing different sounds.

00142629 ....$359.00

tycoon®
PERCUSSION

EXCLUSIVELY DISTRIBUTED BY

HAL•LEONARD®

ce and availability subject to change without notice.

more details and other outstanding cajons, please visit
w.halleonard.com or www.tycoonpercussion.com.

0315

HAL•LEONARD® DRUM PLAY-ALONG

The Drum Play-Along™ Series will help you play your favorite songs quickly and easily! Just follow the drum notation, listen to the audio to hear how the drums should sound, and then play-along using the separate backing tracks. The lyrics are also included for reference. The audio files are enhanced so you can adjust the recording to any tempo without changing pitch!

HAL•LEONARD®

Visit Hal Leonard Online at
www.halleonard.com

Prices, contents and availability subject to change without notice and may vary outside the US.